The Atheists Are Revolting!

Taking back the planet
Saying no to religion

Nick Gisburne

The Atheists Are Revolting!
Published in 2007 by InternetAtheists.com
www.InternetAtheists.com

Copyright © Nick Gisburne 2007
www.gisburne.com

All rights reserved. No part of this book may be reproduced or transmitted in any form or by any means, electronic or mechanical, including photocopying, recording, or by any information storage and retrieval system, without permission in writing from the copyright owner, Nick Gisburne.

ISBN: 978-1-4303-1442-4

Cover Image Credit:
The Blue Marble from Apollo 17
NASA's Visible Earth site
http://visibleearth.nasa.gov/

Contents

Introduction 7
1. Serve God or Burn Forever... 16
2. God or Santa? Same Difference 23
3. WWJD? What Would *You* Do? 26
4. Heaven is a Mental Institution 30
5. Intelligent Design = Creationism 38
6. God Almighty's Genesis Diary – Day 1 41
7. Bible Prophecies Prove Nothing 44
8. What Are You? Some Kind of Atheist? 50
9. 'True' Christians 58
10. 7 More Deadly Sins 67
11. God's Big Test 70
12. Genocide is Never Out of Context 74
13. God Almighty's Genesis Diary – Day 2 78
14. How to Prove There Is No God 81
15. God the Suicidal Con Artist 85
16. Animals Don't Need Bibles 87
17. Preaching Hatred 92
18. The True Meaning of Christmas 96
19. A Sinner from Birth to Grave 99
20. God Almighty's Genesis Diary – Day 3 102
21. Who Do You Think You Are? 106
22. Single Cell to Christian in 6000 Years 110
23. It's Just a Theory 114

24. After-Life Comparisons	121
25. In Cash We Trust	126
26. Fallacies, Lies, Strawmen and Dogma	128
27. God Almighty's Genesis Diary – Day 4	134
28. The Holy Threesome	137
29. Killing for Atheism	139
30. Comparing Christianity to Racism	141
31. Hiding Opinions Behind the Bible	144
32. Cherry Picking, Prejudice and Hate	148
33. Why God Won't Reveal Himself	152
34. God Almighty's Genesis Diary – Day 5	156
35. Biggest Bullshit Bible Story – Part 1	160
36. Biggest Bullshit Bible Story – Part 2	165
37. Biggest Bullshit Bible Story – Part 3	170
38. Flood Fossil Fantasies	179
39. God's Little Retirement Project	184
40. Why is the Bible So Complicated?	189
41. God Almighty's Genesis Diary – Day 6	194
42. God is Irrelevant, Religion is Not	198
43. God's Hard Drive is Bigger Than Yours	203
44. Atheist Poems for Christian Kids	206
45. Christians Need Miracles More Than Atheists Do	208
46. God is History's Biggest Torturer	212
47. God Almighty's Genesis Diary – Day 7	215

For Tara, more than just a friend

Introduction

Call yourself an atheist?

There is no God. If you can say that, you're an atheist. But *would* you say it? Would you tell your colleagues at work that you're not a Christian? How would your boss react to the news? Would you still have a job at the end of the day?

Would you tell your friends at college that you think Heaven does not exist? If you went to a party and the topic changed to religion, would you make a stand and put the case for atheism as forcefully as the Christians in the room would defend their God?

You finally get that hot date, and his/her parents ask you which church you attend. Would you tell them you don't believe in God?

If you said 'no' to any of those questions, you don't need to worry. That worry is guilt, and to an atheist that is no sin at all! But if you said 'no' and *wish* you could say 'yes', maybe this is the book for you.

Atheism is coming out of the closet. Women's rights did it. Anti-racism did it. The gay movement did it. Now it's time for atheists to make a stand, to stand up and be counted. You are *not* part of a small, downtrodden group of people. If you live in an English speaking country (which is where I expect most of my readers will live), atheists already outnumber every religion except one. There are more atheists in the US than Jews. There are more atheists in the UK than Muslims. Only Christians outnumber us. And *they* are the problem.

I am an atheist. I have no belief in any god, which is the basic definition of an atheist. However, unlike some atheists, I will say for the record that I *believe* that the gods of the world's religions do not exist. Purists will say that atheism is not a belief, and I agree that most atheists will wear that hat. But there is such a thing as strong atheism, which is the hat *I* choose to wear. Strong atheists actively deny the existence of gods. They speak out. The fact that I believe that those gods do not exist is just semantics. I have no belief that they do exist, while at the same time believing that they don't exist. I've heard of them, and I believe that what has been described to me is bullshit. That simple statement is not a belief *system* and it's not by any means a religion, but my atheism is what it is – a strong affirmation that no supernatural being exists, or indeed has ever existed.

I am sure that the God of the Bible does not exist. 100% sure? Well, maybe the same percentage as the certainty that the tooth fairy does not exist. There's always the chance that I'm wrong, but I stopped believing in the tooth fairy when I put a tooth under my pillow without telling my mother I'd done it. Next morning, no cash, and the tooth was still there. I became a tooth fairy atheist. At the age of six I'd weighed up the evidence, found it lacking, and lost my faith in the magic.

Christianity is a bigger tooth to pull. One third of the world's population believe that Jesus Christ died on a wooden cross and rose up to Heaven. A Heaven where people who have already died live again, happily ever after. The fairy tale ending was intentional, I assure you, because this is what modern religion is – a fairy tale, a tall story, a series of ancient myths and legends every bit as fantastical as those written about Zeus, Anubis, and Quetzalcoatl. But Christianity is a fairy tale believed by grown ups, people living in the 21st century, and this sets it apart from the average myth.

Religion in Europe has largely been put out to pasture. I live in the UK, where the Anglican Church, here called the Church of England, is the *official* state religion. Yet almost nobody goes to church here. British Christianity lives up to its image of the old fashioned Sunday service – solemn hymns and tea with the vicar. It is no longer relevant to 95% of the population, and of the 5% who do attend regularly, you will find few people who are outspoken about their faith, fewer still who are active in the way that many American Christians have now become active. The picture is similar throughout the 'Christian world', in all but one country.

The USA, uniquely among all the nations of the world where Christianity is the majority religion, has become a crucible for Christian political ambition. Quite literally, the Christians are taking over, or at least making a damned good attempt at doing so. Religion *is* politics in the US. If you are a Fundamentalist Christian, it's a pretty safe bet you'll vote Republican. If you're an atheist, you couldn't get anyone to *take* the bet that you'll call yourself a Democrat.

The mega-churches of the Christian heartlands, when pooled together, hold tremendous political influence. They are organised. They can mobilise people behind a political cause. They can get 20,000 people marching in front of an abortion clinic. They can raise a million dollars to support the campaign of a senator who will promote an anti-gay agenda.

It is the Fundamentalist Christians who are perhaps the most active in politics. Their agenda is clear: get into government and turn the United States into a Christian theocracy. But, and there is a 'but' here, the Fundamentalist Christians, like the atheists, are *not* the majority. *Most* Christians do not believe that the world is 6000 years old and that the dinosaurs went onto Noah's Ark. *Many* Christians are pro-choice. *Many* Christians support civil partnerships for gay couples (legal throughout the UK already). And *many* Christians also have the same values held by many atheists. If only their belief in God didn't get in the way!

Why do I care about American Christians? 10 years ago I never even considered that the religious make-up of the USA was any different from the rest of the civilised world. I assumed that Christianity was fading into obscurity. But when George W Bush says that God told him to invade Iraq, that starts to involve me, because the UK was swept up in the same disastrous Iraq war. A religious war, Christian nation versus Muslim nation(s).

When British people start to die, when British money starts to pour out of the country into arms, instead of into schools and hospitals, that's when US religion starts to affect me. When Bush vetoes an important stem cell research bill because otherwise the religious right would never forgive him, that's when US religion becomes important to me. When American 'End Timers' are so vocal about the world coming to an end when Jesus comes back to 'Rapture' the Christians up to Heaven, and as a result they don't give a shit about global warming or the conservation of scarce resources, that's when Christianity starts to look like it's getting a little too big for its boots.

For several months, from late 2006 and into 2007, I made a series of personal videos, discussing atheism and religion. I posted them on the YouTube web site, under the name Gisburne2000, and later used my full name, Nick Gisburne. People watched them. They were popular. More importantly, it became apparent that YouTube (which had itself only been running for around 18 months) was building up a growing number of atheist video bloggers. These were ordinary people, of all ages, from all around the world. No two atheists were alike, but the feeling of community spirit was obvious. Organising atheists has been likened to herding cats – when people are united only by an absence of belief, what is there to bring them together? YouTube was one thing which seemed able to do that.

When I left at the end of 2006 (YouTube had become so addictive that I needed a break), this only served to prove that not believing in an invisible man cannot in itself motivate you to take action. However, I *was* motivated, and indeed I *am* motivated, to continue to share my thoughts with other atheists. This is why I wrote the book you are now reading.

The biggest thing we have as atheists is not our organisation. It is our numbers. Everywhere you look there are atheists. But many won't come out and tell you this because in many places it is not considered acceptable or appropriate to deny the existence of God. This must change.

This book is my attempt at motivating atheists, to help them tell their friends, their colleagues, everyone they can, that they are the same person as before, but no part of that person is in any way religious. You don't believe the nonsense that is Christianity (or any other religion), so you should not feel inhibited about telling people as much.

And, just as importantly, I want this book to give atheists the ammunition they need to explain *why* Christianity is not the great, all-loving religion it's made out to be.

There's bad news: you might have to read the Bible. Because if you don't know all the bad parts (from the Christian point of view) you'll only hear the good parts (the ones they read out in church) from the Christians who talk to you. So try to read beyond what the Christians tell you is proof of 'God's love', and root out the fallacies, the double standards, and the hatred. It's all in there, and in fact the Bible is probably the atheist's greatest weapon when justifying the rejection of Christianity. You may soon find that if Christians understood what the Bible is *really* saying, there would be many more atheists and far fewer Christians!

This book does not have the scholarship of Richard Dawkins or Sam Harris to commend it. I will not delve into philosophy or metaphysics. I am not a scientist, so I will only dig into evolution or astronomy deeply enough to make my point.

Unlike most other atheist books you may have read, I will not hesitate to use profanity as and when I think it has a place! 'Bad' language is still language, and to give an example, I know of no better word for irrational religious dogma than 'bullshit', so let me use it without further delay:

This is my attempt to show that religion deserves no more respect than your support for a particular sports team, or your preference for one soft drink over another. Religion is still seen as a taboo subject for satire, but we should not be afraid to speak out about it, to make light of it, to disrespect every aspect of it. Religion is fiction, it is myth... it is, in fact, complete bullshit. What respect should we have for a religion that does not respect our right to be critical of its teachings?

Some of the essays in this book may seem trivial or nonsensical. But remember that Christians have based their whole lives on a book of unproven stories from history. Sometimes comparing God with Santa Claus is the only way to make Christians understand that their stories are just as fanciful and far-fetched as the man in the moon.

Use this book as a starting point for discussion with other atheists... and with Christians when you're feeling brave! I have endeavoured to steer away from the tried and tested route of finding faults and contradictions in specific Bible passages, though inevitably some are mentioned. There are many other sources that do so extremely well, and far more comprehensively than I could. Some advice: the one thing you really should avoid is trading scripture quotes with a Christian – therein lies the path to madness!

The trick is to know the routes that Christians will take with their arguments, and avoid those places. They will have heard the standard rebuttals and will quickly return their own routine arguments, inevitably ending in stalemate. Although you will read about this later in the book, here is a little taster of one approach you can try.

A Christian will tell you that the Universe is so complex that it could not possibly have come about by chance. It *must* have been created by God. You just have to look at the Universe to realise that this is true. That may be his whole argument, his 'proof' for God's existence.

When presented with this splendid piece of nonsense, what you have is a person telling you that 'nobody knows how the Universe was created, so we made something up.' Already you have won the argument.

Point out to him that if the Universe is so vast and so complex, surely *one* god wouldn't be enough? Maybe there are two gods. Or twenty. Or a thousand. Maybe the Universe is so complex that there are gods everywhere. After all, if the only reason he is giving for God is that by looking at the Universe you can just know, it stands to reason that there *must* be more than one god. Doesn't it? Can't he see that? Doesn't he know?

That initial look of bewilderment is priceless, and when he realises that he now has to disprove a second god in exactly the same way that he wanted you to disprove the first, there's very little he can do about it. Of course after a moment's thought he will almost certainly return to 'special pleading', but the argument will already have been won.

February 2007

Banned from YouTube.

This book should have been published in February 2007, and I returned to YouTube early in that month, blowing off the cobwebs of my video channel there, ready to make an announcement.

Unfortunately YouTube had other ideas.

Very early on in my YouTube 'life' I had made a couple of slideshows containing some of the 'bad' passages from the Bible and, importantly, the Qur'an. On 9 February the Qur'an video was flagged as 'Inappropriate Content' and removed. Worse, because I had had two earlier 'offences', YouTube deemed it necessary to not only pull that video but to remove *every* video from my account. Finally they deleted the account itself. Every trace of my channel was gone.

For someone who was days away from announcing an atheist book to around 500 subscribers, people already interested in what I had to say, this was devastating.

I made a video asking for support from fellow atheists, urging them to contact YouTube to restore my account, and created a new account from which it could be seen. Since the 'banned' video was flagged as 'Inappropriate Content' this quickly became an issue of censorship. Why was YouTube removing a video critical of Islam (the only video of mine with such content) and yet leaving alone a very similar video presenting unfavourable Christian Bible passages?

These things escalate very quickly indeed. Three days later I had over 1300 subscribers as the news spread that a video critical of Islam had been censored. The story was featured on Slashdot, Digg and hundreds of blogs around the world. Scores of video responses to my request for help put that video within a hair's breadth of the top 20 most responded videos on YouTube *of all time*. Everybody was talking about it.

Introduction 13

In protest at the apparent censorship, I and my supporters re-posted the 'banned' video again, on many different channels, and I also put it alongside the Bible quotes video. If one was deleted but the other remained, that would be a clear indication that speaking out against Christianity was allowed, while showing Islam in a negative light was subject to strict censorship.

Sure enough, on 11 February, two days after my original account had been closed, the Qur'an video was pulled by YouTube again, and the reason was given as 'Rejected (content inappropriate)'. The Bible quotes video was left untouched.

This of course added fresh fuel to the flames, and further calls for YouTube to restore my original channel were made. They were all ignored.

On 12 February 2007 the story changed. YouTube changed it. I received an email telling me that the video had not been removed for 'inappropriate content' but for 'copyright infringement'. When I made a video to tell people this, of course nobody believed it – this was plainly seen as some kind of cover-up, some way of removing me from YouTube quietly (too late!) using the rather less controversial excuse of copyright infringement.

The Qur'an video did contain audio used without permission from the copyright holders. But so did the Bible quotes video. So do hundreds of thousands of videos all over YouTube. If you removed all such audio from YouTube there would remain only a small fraction of the videos on the web site. This still looked like censorship.

It looked a lot worse later that day when YouTube closed the new account. I had by now re-uploaded 20 of my old videos, which were again deleted. The subscriptions I had built up, over 1300, were gone. Everything was totally erased, for the second time.

Furthermore, YouTube sent me an email citing the DMCA (Digital Millennium Copyright Act) which, they said, required them to delete not only the original account, but also the new account. The message was clear: I was not only deleted from YouTube, but since any new account would be deleted that meant that I was effectively *banned* from posting videos on YouTube ever again.

The bottom line is that the offending video *was* removed for copyright reasons. YouTube forwarded to me a copy of the DMCA notice they had received from the owners of the music, and it was clear that I had crossed the line. Since I had done this twice before already (I had re-posted clips of a Richard Dawkins documentary and also a TV interview of Richard Dawkins), my three 'strikes' were up, and I was out.

Of course, the poor way in which this was handled by YouTube fuelled a conspiracy theory of huge proportions, which will probably continue indefinitely. People still believe the video was censored because of its content, rather than for copyright reasons. They don't even believe *me* when I tell them the real reasons!

This still left me with no access to posting videos on YouTube, and with a finished book to publicise. But the solution was obvious: if I couldn't post my own videos, other people would. As I write, there are over 60 different channels on YouTube hosting my atheist videos. In total there are over 500 videos, obviously including multiple copies. I now have ten times the presence on YouTube that was the case before this all started.

If there is one thing that atheists are able to do when one of their own is targeted, it is rally round to help, and I want to offer up a personal tribute to each and every person who uploaded my videos, made their own protest video, wrote to YouTube, or simply sent me an email in support. I am truly astounded by the scale of the encouragement I continue to receive.

I am the atheist they banned from YouTube. But I am every bit a part of that vital community which has come to be known as the 'YouTube atheists'. This book is for them, but it is also addressed to the wider audience, one which goes beyond YouTube and the confines of the Internet. I would like to see more people write articles or books about their own experiences with atheism, and their struggles against the ridiculous prejudice and downright hatred that many religious believers have for atheists and atheism.

This book was hard work, but here it is. I challenge you to write your own, possible even collaborate in a joint venture, and be part of a growing voice for atheism. But if not, try not to be silent the next time you hear the bigotry of the type of Christian who promotes belief in God over the welfare and happiness of living human beings. People are still persecuted in the name of religion, and in the 21st century this simply should not be the case.

My recent experiences proved to me that atheists are certainly a force to be reckoned with. Christians aren't the only ones who can mobilise in support of a cause. In the face of fierce religious condemnation, the atheists are truly revolting!

March 2007

The word of God.

As an atheist I have no belief in any god, but in this book I frequently capitalise the word 'God', which some may view as affording the Christian god far too much respect. This is not the case. Calling the god of the Bible 'God' is simply shorthand, and implies nothing. It is, after all, simply the name given to him by Christians. If I say 'god' I mean 'any god you care to mention'. If I say 'God' I mean 'the god of Christianity, Islam and Judaism'.

Other words, such as 'Heaven' or 'Hell', refer to well-known religious places, events or objects. No additional respect is implied or given.

Of course the word 'atheist' is never capitalised. Atheism is not a religion, it's not even an organisation. It's just a simple description of our absence of belief in any god, or gods.

The YouTube Atheists.

To my friends on YouTube who have encouraged me, criticised me and kept me going through some pretty tough times, a special message to you: thanks! Okay, so it wasn't *that* special, but you know how bad I am at this kind of thing – I'll open a few cans of beer in your honour, how's that?

Cheers!

Nick Gisburne

1

Serve God or Burn Forever

God is not love. God is threats.

I've had an idea. I've had an idea that God might have more followers in the following scenario:

The Bible says words to this effect: 'Believe in God, worship God, and you will go to Heaven and be rewarded with eternal life.' Sounds great doesn't it? Sounds pretty good so far. It's a good deal.

What if the Bible also said, 'If you don't worship me, you'll not go to Heaven, but God will not punish you. You'll just die, and that will be the end of you. You will cease to exist.' So, no big problem, because that is exactly what atheists believe will happen anyway.

So far, we can all take Heaven or leave it. You won't suffer, you'll just lose the chance to go there. That's the deal you make, the choice you have to live with.

In my opinion, if this was what the Bible taught us, if Christianity was a choice we could make freely, without fear of the consequences, more people would turn to God.

Unfortunately this is *not* what the Bible teaches. What Christians believe is that, yes, if you believe in God, if you worship God, you will go to Heaven. Again, that's great, cool. It's fine. If that's what you want to do, you'll go to Heaven and have a great time.

However, if you *don't* worship God you will burn in Hell, in eternal torment, in a lake of fire. Suddenly this doesn't sound so appealing! Eternal means forever. Not just a hundred years, but *billions* of years. Forever is a long, long time.

We can summarise God's intentions here very simply:
Serve me or burn.
In other words, this is a threat. What else could it be?

Any religion which relies on threatening, abusive teachings (and this *is* abusive: 'love me or you will be punished'), is clearly a religion which cannot have goodness at the heart of its teachings. Threats are unacceptable. This is a threat. It is wrong.

Imagine a wedding ceremony. The groom is happy, loving, smiling, and he turns to his beautiful bride to tell her, 'I promise to love you, to honour you, to be faithful to you... but if you step out of line I will hack you to pieces and torture you with rusty razor blades *forever.*'

Is this love? Clearly not.

Evil dictators throughout history are too numerous to count, but let's mention a few: Hitler, Stalin, Saddam Hussein. What did they do when people didn't agree with them? They put all the dissenters to death, or into punishment camps, maybe tortured them, tortured their relatives, their friends, purely because they disagreed or did not obey the rules of the dictatorship.

Does this principle sound familiar? Does it not sound more than a little like God sending people to Hell for failing to be a faithful servant? In fact it sounds *exactly* like that.

God will send you to Hell if you do not follow him. This is one of the principle teachings of Christianity. Love God and you will go to Heaven. If not, God himself will send you to Hell. God made Hell for exactly this purpose, and he will send you there.

God does not love you unconditionally. Certainly, God loves you when you love him, but if you don't love God, clearly God hates you enough to punish you, for all eternity. He doesn't like it when you don't do what he says. He will punish you, and the punishment will last for all time (hardly a punishment to fit the crime, *any* crime), if you don't serve him.

Is this a good God? Is this a loving God? Or is this a vindictive, nasty, evil God? I doubt if you need to be given the answers to these questions, because from this description the reality is clear to see.

Bad Christians go to Heaven. Good atheists burn forever.

So already we can see that the Bible teaches that if you don't love God you will burn in eternal torment in a lake of fire, in Hell. Your skin will be roasted, toasted and flipped on an everlasting barbecue, just for that big old sin of not believing in God.

It's interesting to see the reaction from Christians when you put this to them. Most are of the opinion that God doesn't hate the sinner, but he *really* hates the sin, and you must be punished for those sins.

It's like a judge sending a murderer to prison. Bad people have to be punished.

On the surface this sounds fair enough. All countries have their own justice systems, so you could expect God to have one too. If you do bad things you go to Hell. There does seem to be a faint thread of logic there somewhere.

But let's analyse the reality of the situation again: if you sin, God will punish you for it. He hates that sin, he really does. So if that's the case, why can a truly *bad* Christian, who may have sinned all his life, but repented near its end, manage to escape from punishment?

If you are a rapist, if you are a murderer, if you are an abuser of children, and yet you find God, accept Jesus into your heart and *repent*, guess what?

God will forgive you!

In fact God will forgive you for *anything*, as long as you believe in him and worship him at the time of your death.

Understand that I'm not talking about someone who purposefully plans to do this, to commit crimes and then produce a 'get out of Hell free card' on his death bed. Obviously the repentance would have to be genuine – God the mind-reader would know if you were trying to trick him.

Nevertheless, the fact remains that a simple 'sorry' will get you a free pass to eternal bliss, and all your crimes, all your evil deeds, everything will go unpunished, completely wiped away. Do anything you like, then repent, without so much as a slap on the wrist.

So what happened to this big hater of sins? If you're a Christian are you immune to God's one-punishment-fits-all justice system?

And meanwhile, where are the atheists in God's master plan?

Let's take a sample atheist. A good atheist. There are good people of all religions, certainly, and there are bad people. There are good atheists and bad. It is human nature. We all do things we shouldn't. But for this example, we'll look at the life of a good atheist.

The good atheist came from a decent home, a good family background. She worked hard at school and grew up into a fine adult. She earned a place in medical school on merit, became a doctor, then a surgeon. She saved hundreds of lives, even became a pioneer in certain aspects of modern surgery. She wrote papers, taught others to follow in her footsteps. She made her mark on her profession.

Beyond work, she eventually married, and with her husband raised a couple of children. Those kids were taught right from wrong. They were taught to value friendship, to respect other people's views, but to be unafraid to give their own opinions. Like the mother, her children grew up to be fine adults, good citizens, decent people.

The woman was loved by her husband, her children and eventually her grandchildren. She was respected by colleagues and friends. She lived a happy, successful life. Inevitably, her life ended. She died in the arms of her family, who respected her wishes for a non-religious funeral. Her body was buried and her family cherished her memory.

All except those Christians who knew she was an atheist. Those Christians mourned her passing, but for them the tragedy was worse. Because they knew that this woman, this good, kind, caring doctor, was in Hell, screaming in agony, her body burning in unending pain, and she would remain there, without relief, for a billion years and beyond.

Why? Well of course, she didn't believe in God, so it was only fair that she should be tortured wasn't it?

This is the bullshit reality of Biblical sin, repentance and punishment. God doesn't hate sin. The only thing he hates is people who don't believe in him. That's it. That is the bottom line. There is *nothing* more important to the Christian God than worship by the faithful. Repent and you *will* be forgiven.

Imagine a scene in court. Ted Bundy, who raped and murdered scores of young women across the United States in the 1970s, steps up to the judge. The judge tells him, 'Ted Bundy, you have been sentenced to death for the murder of dozens of innocent people. These are terrible crimes and you must pay. Do you have any final words before you are taken away?'

Bundy says, 'Er, well... sorry.'

The judge frowns. 'You're sorry?'

Bundy nods. 'Definitely. I wish I'd never done it. I was wrong and I'm truly sorry. Please forgive me. I am *so* sorry.'

The judge thinks for a minute, and looks right into Bundy's eyes. He can see that Bundy is genuinely repentant. So he shrugs and says, 'Right. Okay then. If you're sorry I'll let you go. Now just you behave yourself okay?'

One of the most notorious mass murderers in history goes free, all because the person in charge of dealing out justice knew that he was sorry for what he'd done. In the same way, if he accepts Jesus into his life, he will go to Heaven.

Meanwhile, the good doctor is roasting in the fire, in an indestructible body which will never die, and will always feel the worst kind of pain. She didn't murder anyone, in fact she *saved* lives, but that is of no consequence to the Christian God. There is no mercy for a non-believer.

The essence of this is that not only does God forgive people who sin, he *punishes* good, decent, honest people, whose only fault is that they don't believe in him. Is this a good God, or is this an evil, malicious God who wants to punish people *solely* for the 'crime' of non-belief and turns a blind eye to crime so long as he is worshipped?

Consider these two questions:

- Is there anything that anyone can do, by their actions, their words, their thoughts, to avoid going to Hell, other than accepting Jesus into their hearts?

- Is there anything that anyone can do, by their actions, their words, their thoughts, which would be so bad it would disqualify them from Heaven if, after all they have done, they decide to accept Jesus into their hearts?

If the answer to both these questions is 'no', and many Christians will tell you, without flinching, that this is what they believe, this means that there is only *one* sin, that of non-belief. Nothing else matters. What kind of immoral justice system would give Adolf Hitler and the Dalai Lama, or Gandhi, the same punishment? What kind of immoral justice system would reward rapists and paedophiles in the blink of an eye, simply because they were 'saved'?

Such an unfair, immoral, *evil* system of justice is preached, loudly and proudly, by Christianity.

Remember that if you're an atheist you do not *choose* to be an atheist, even if you've become an atheist and were once a Christian. Atheists simply have no belief in God. This is not a choice. It just happens. If someone told you to believe in Zeus, could you do it? Belief in the Christian God is no different.

Yet the Bible is being used to teach Christians that whatever you've done, however bad you are, God will forgive you. Meanwhile, atheists are just fuel for the fire, regardless of their conduct, and despite the fact that they may lead 'better' lives than many Christians.

This makes me happy to be an atheist. I wouldn't want a God who punishes for one crime and one crime only: not loving him. That is the sin that will get you to Hell. Not rape, murder, or genocide. Nothing else will get you to Hell quicker than not loving God.

Is this really the kind of religion that people should be teaching to their families? Christianity is teaching children that their atheist friends will be tortured. Believe in God, boys and girls, or you'll burn in Hell. That's how much he loves you.

God's 'love' is abusive.

A while ago I received a message from a Christian who had listened to the arguments I've given you in this section, and yet still didn't seem to understand the points I'd made about burning in Hell if you don't love Jesus.

He told me that praising God and Jesus isn't the least bit threatening. In fact, it's more like a teacher who gives you some notes and says, 'if you study this you will pass your test, but if you don't study this you will fail.'

He made it clear that in his eyes loving God and Jesus is a choice.

I was dumbfounded. How is the example he gave even *remotely* comparable?

What if the teacher had said, 'study and you'll pass, but if you don't study *I will roast you over an open fire forever, while you scream in unending pain*'?

The teacher and study analogy doesn't even begin to cover it. The consequences aren't anywhere near as bad. You don't feel physically and mentally *threatened* by the thought of failing a test.

However you *should* feel threatened, and probably *would* feel threatened, if someone told you that you will be tortured if you don't love them.

Let's put this another way:

A father tells all his children that he loves them, but that he doesn't love the bad things they do. 'Do you love me too?' he asks his children. 'Of course we do,' they say.

Then the father adds, 'Don't forget, if you stop loving me I will burn you with this cigarette'.

The Christian could not equate this with the Bible's philosophy, but to an atheist like myself this is self-evident. When does 'love' start to become abuse? When the consequences become serious enough to cause actual harm to a person, either physically or mentally.

There are many, many atheists who used to be Christians but who ended up realising that Christianity had made them into fearful people, afraid to do *anything* in case they offended God. That is mental abuse. It's damaging, and it's what religion can do to people.

It is brainwashing, conditioning of the mind to behave in a certain way. Putting fear of harmful consequences into someone's head can crush a person's spirit and paralyse them with fear, almost as easily as waving a knife in front of their face. Unlike the knife, it's all in your mind, so it is much harder to make the effects of mental threats go away.

The same Christian said to me that Christianity is like friendship, not threatening at all. If you bribe someone, or threaten them, or force them to be your friend, there wouldn't be a real friendship. God wants your love, so he cannot be threatening anyone.

But he immediately went on to say, 'when we choose something else but God, we automatically choose Hell'.

How is that a free choice? What if I said to you, 'You can be my friend, but if you don't *choose* to be my friend, if you choose something else, you automatically choose to be burned to death'?

I am constantly amazed that Christians do not see this. They refuse to even look at the possibility that Christianity is all about threats. This is a point that must be constantly rammed home:

If you are given two choices and one of those choices is torture for all eternity, that is a *threat*. What else could it possibly be?

One final comparison. Think of a woman, bruised and battered by her abusive husband, yet unable to see the truth. 'He loves me,' she will say, 'he only does these things because he loves me.'

Christians need to realise what their religion is teaching them. In among the 'God is love' slogans, buried so deep that somehow only non-Christians can see them, are the real messages of Christianity:

- God is not love. God is threats.
- Bad Christians go to Heaven.
- Good atheists burn forever.
- God's 'love' is abusive.

The next time a Christian says, 'God loves you', just remind him what his religion teaches that God will do if you don't return that love. If you fall out of love with your partner, you will both go your separate ways without further incident. But if you fall out of love with God, welcome to pain without end.

2

God or Santa? Same Difference

Convincing an Evangelist? Possible!

If you've ever tried to explain to an Evangelical Christian that you don't believe in God, and that atheism is not, in fact, denial of a God you know exists, but is actually an absence of any belief at all, you'll know that it's as futile as trying to convince the sea that it should stop waving at you.

But all is not lost. The following story has worked at least once. An atheist contacted me and told me that his fiancée, a devout Christian (sadly I sense compatibility issues somewhere down the line!), had constantly brought up Christianity, not understanding why he could not see the 'truth' about God and the Bible. His protests that it was all just silly stories fell on deaf ears. She simply could not grasp the concept that her religion meant so little to an atheist.

After listening to this story, she finally understood, and she promised never to raise the issue again. Result!

Evangelists should note that there is no point telling an atheist that we must ask to be 'forgiven' for the sin of not believing in God. For one thing, if you don't believe in something, how can you then suddenly believe in it without any evidence? I can't ask to be forgiven for not believing, when it's not my fault that I don't believe. Even if I wanted to believe (I don't), I could no more believe in God than I could believe in dragons and elves.

And who would I be asking for forgiveness? Oh God, who I don't believe in, please forgive me for not believing in you. I know you won't answer because I don't believe in you, but... you get the idea. That's just the way it is. It's impossible for an atheist to believe in God.

What I'm going to do is give you an analogy. I want to show you what Christianity, that collection of impossible stories in the Bible, sounds like to an atheist.

The story I'm about to tell will seem ridiculous, but that's how an atheist sees the fanciful stories written in the Bible. All I'll do is change the names. Everything else will stay the same... kind of!

What Christianity sounds like to an atheist.

Santa Claus loves you.

Santa sent his only begotten reindeer, Rudolph, to forgive you your sins. If you will just believe in Santa you will have eternal life at the North Pole... somewhere nice and warm, with a cosy fire.

All you need to do is accept that you are a sinner. Just make a list of all your sins, check it twice, and Santa will hear you. Because, as it is written, Santa knows who's been naughty and who's been nice. When you believe in Santa, and turn your face to Rudolph, all your sins will be forgiven.

We are all Santa's little helpers, and we can all spread the good news about Santa. But if you turn away from Santa, your presents will be taken from you and roasted forever, along with the chestnuts, on an open fire. For Santa is a jealous old man, with a bit of a weight problem.

But he just wants you to love him.

It hurts Santa when atheists don't believe in him. He wants to love you, but if you don't love Santa you will have to be punished. Santa punishes those who don't believe in him – you won't get *any* presents again, for all eternity.

Atheists say that Santa doesn't exist, but we can prove it. The good book, the Giant Book of Fairy Stories and Nursery Rhymes, tells how Santa made all the toys in six days. And on the seventh day he put down his tools and had a bit of a rest, and probably a glass of sherry and a mince pie.

The Old Book of Christmas prophesied that a man would come down from the skies, and he would be wearing a red costume and a big beard, and he would bring gifts from the north. And it came to pass – that's exactly what happened.

And if it hadn't come to pass we would have written it down so that it sounded that way anyway.

Santa came down at night, down every chimney in the world, and left presents for all mankind. And he took all the mince pies that had been left for him, just to keep him going on the return trip.

And yea, Santa's only begotten reindeer passed among the land of men, and did great things, which we call miracles.

Rudolph walked on water, but as it was winter it had turned to ice – because you can't really walk on water, that would be silly! But Rudolph wasn't a very good skater, so Thumper the rabbit had to help him. And it was good.

Then the reindeer fed 5000 people, with only two bales of straw and a box of oats. And that was good too.

But in the end, the fire in the forest got out of hand and a hunter killed Rudolph with a rifle, and that was sad, but it was all in the prophecies, so that made it okay.

And Santa took Rudolph's body up onto his sleigh, back to the North Pole, and put a bandage on the bullet-hole, and he was better in no time.

But the day is coming when Santa Claus *will* return. The Giant Book of Stories says that Santa Claus *is* coming to town, so you have to believe it.

It was all written in the magic book, and that is the word of Santa, and the word of Santa is the truth, and you can't argue because there's all kinds of other stuff in there that we'll use to confuse you if you try to outsmart us.

When Santa comes again, all those who believe in him will be taken up on his magic sleigh and transported to the North Pole. And all those who don't have faith in him will have to watch re-runs of old movies on TV for all eternity.

In the name of the Father (Christmas), the reindeer and the holly branch, this is the truth and the light, and if you don't believe it, don't say we didn't warn you.

Amen. Or as it says in the good book: ho ho ho.

3

WWJD? What Would *You* Do?

A new situation.

This is a question for Christians as well as atheists. Atheists will find this easy, but it's a question you should put to your Christian friends as often as possible. They may find it difficult to keep their 'morals only come from the Bible' stance, while at the same time admitting that atheists can make the right choices too.

Christians first need to be made aware that they will have to do some serious, hard thinking. You are going to ask them to imagine a situation, and I want them to think about it carefully, and come up with an answer.

Don't allow them to say, 'That's a hypothetical situation and it would never happen'. That's the point. This is a 'what if', designed to make them think. And if they can't think beyond what they already know, or think they know because it's what their faith tells them, if they are unable to, or refuse to imagine what you are about to ask them, then they have already confirmed what atheists think about religion.

Read out the following passage to your Christian friends:

What would *you* do?

Imagine that *you* are an atheist. Imagine that you don't believe in God, in the Bible, in Jesus Christ, or any of the other gods or religions there might be in the world. Imagine you are 100% atheist. You're not even agnostic, you are certain in your mind that there is no

God. Imagine that you've always been this way, that there has never been a time when you haven't been an atheist.

Okay, now answer me this question. Knowing yourself, knowing who you are, and remembering that you have put yourself in the position of a non-believer, what is stopping you now from going out onto the street and murdering someone? What's stopping you from robbing the first person you see on the street when you go out?

I don't mean the police; I mean what is it inside your mind that tells you that these things are wrong? Because now you don't have the option of saying 'What would Jesus do?'. The only fall-back you have is, 'What would *you* do?'

If the answer is that you are fearful of the consequences, that you might get caught and punished by the law, is that the real reason you don't go out and commit the crime? Would you kill someone if you knew you could get away with it?

Or do you restrain yourself, or probably don't even get the urge at all, because you don't want other people to suffer because of your actions? Or perhaps because you know that these things are simply wrong?

Imagine that you're passing someone on the street, someone who's just lying there. Their head is bleeding. They're unconscious. They look in a bad way. What would you do? Remember that you don't believe in God, you believe that there's nobody up there watching you, so in theory there are no consequences if you just walk right on down the street and do nothing. Nobody will ever know if you let this person bleed to death.

But what would you do, if you personally did not believe in God?

Basic questions.

These are very basic questions, basic moral questions. And they are questions that Christians ask of atheists every day. Not directly, certainly. No Christian will ask an atheist 'how come you didn't kill someone today?' because if they did, the Christian would soon realise that it's not the Bible telling an atheist to live a good, moral life. So it must be something else.

Christians like to assert that the Bible is the only source of human morality. Without the Bible, we would all descend into anarchy. We would all become immoral. We would lie, cheat, steal, even kill without the lessons of the Bible. The Bible gives Christians the moral code which forms the basis of their everyday behaviour. What would we do without it?

Well personally I wouldn't want to kill someone or rob them, because I simply have no desire to do so. I know it's wrong. I know that if everybody did it, pretty soon only the ones with the bigger guns or the better aim would survive. I don't want to kill anybody, and in return I don't want anyone to kill me. We'd have no society at all if we all went around killing each other.

And after helping the person bleeding on the street, I might think to myself 'that could have been me. I hope someone helps me if I'm ever hurt'.

Of course the main reason for assisting someone in distress is empathy, the ability to relate to someone else's suffering. Knowing, or at least being able to imagine, the pain felt by the wounded person, even if they are a complete stranger, is a quality found in all humans, to a greater or lesser extent. It is of course also found in animals, and I will discuss that elsewhere in this book.

And yet, I don't believe in God. I don't *have* to be considerate. No book is telling me to feel empathy for anyone. I don't believe there are consequences in the after-life. But like most people, I believe that we should all live a good life and help people if help is needed.

Turning the tables.

Okay, let's assume that now *you* believe in God. This time it's atheists who have to stretch their imagination a little. You believe that God will punish you if you sin. You believe that the Bible shows you how to live your life in a good, clean, moral way.

You don't kill, or steal. You'd help a dying man in the street. What would Jesus do? He'd do the same things, of course. Jesus even spoke of the parable of the good Samaritan.

But wait a minute. When the Christian imagined he was an atheist, he wasn't tempted to kill or steal. He'd have called an ambulance for the person bleeding in the street. So he didn't need the Bible to tell him to do that.

At least I hope not. I hope that the only reason that Christians are not murderers isn't that they believe in God, and that he has commanded them not to kill anyone. If that was the *only* reason preventing a religious person gunning someone down, what would that tell us about their ability to control their own actions?

It was within him to make that choice for himself. It was within him to make moral decisions of his own. Neither the Christian nor the atheist needed a religious book to tell them how to live their lives. Even if they didn't believe in God, Christians would *still* make the same decisions.

People who don't believe in God make the right choices every day. If you want to call that decision process 'good moral values', then it's obvious that it's possible for atheists to have good moral values. And it's possible for *anyone* to make the right choices without thinking 'What would Jesus do?'. It's not Jesus who's responsible for your actions, it's you.

Where exactly does the Bible fit into these moral dilemmas? Does it have a place at all? The very next time a Christian tells you he has acted in a moral way, and mentions that the Bible helped him come to that decision, ask him this question: 'What would an atheist have done in exactly the same circumstances?' If the person knows you well enough, ask him what he thinks you would have done. It may genuinely surprise him to realise that someone who has no belief in God, has no sense of duty to, or respect for, the content of the Bible, would come to precisely the same decision as a Christian.

What would Jesus do? You don't need religion to answer that question. You don't even need to ask the question at all. When confronted with a question of morals, the only thing to ask yourself is 'what would *you* do?' There is no God, so the only person with the ability to answer it is you.

4

Heaven is a Mental Institution

What is your purpose in life?

Christians talk a lot about Heaven. If you're saved by the love of Jesus, Heaven is where you're headed, apparently. But I've talked with enough Christians to realise that they have absolutely no idea what is going on up there.

Atheists are often asked, 'If you don't believe in God, and you don't believe you'll get to Heaven, is there any point to your life? Why do you exist at all?' It seems that Christians really do need a purpose in their lives, and getting to Heaven is it.

> The purpose of life is to glorify God and go to Heaven… 'cause Heaven is our home.
> *Ted Haggard*
> *(that great role model for Christian tolerance!)*

Pastor Rick Warren's *Purpose Driven Life* says you were:
  Planned for God's pleasure   (Worship)
  Formed for God's family   (Fellowship)
  Created to become like Christ (Discipleship)
  Shaped for serving God   (Ministry)
  Made for a mission   (Evangelism)

No 'me' time at all apparently, so any hobbies you might have better be Christian-friendly. Say goodbye to stamp collecting (some of those stamps come from Muslim countries!), but say hello to making anti-gay banners. No time to fix your car, when you should be out there putting pressure on local schools to teach intelligent design in the science class.

These are the important things for Christians. This is what you should do with your life. It's what will get you to Heaven. But maybe you're still not clear what you'll find when you get there.

What is Heaven?

Most sources suggest that a Christian's purpose on Earth seems to be simply to serve God and get to Heaven. So what is Heaven?

> No tears, no mourning, no suffering. It's eternal joy and happiness because you are at one with God.
> *Rev. Dr. Calvin Butts*

> I always think of Heaven as being a place where we won't have any troubles anymore. Heaven is a place where there will be peace and tranquillity.
> *Cardinal Theodore McCarrick*
> *Archbishop of Washington*

> There will be no more death or mourning or crying or pain, for the old order of things has passed away.
> *God (Revelation 21:4)*

So Heaven is basically a place without pain and suffering, with no troubles at all. But what this basically means is that the people in Heaven will be living for a million, billion, trillion years with absolutely no purpose whatsoever.

You won't have to work, because going to work implies getting paid to work, either in money or food or possessions, and because there's no pain and suffering why would you need money or food? God's not going to allow you to starve is he? And it's going to be difficult to die if you're already dead.

You won't have to have sex because that would imply giving birth to new life, and God could just take care of the whole process for you anyway (he has a thing for virgins, apparently). There will be no joy of childbirth because bearing children is painful and messy and hard work. No kids to look after in Heaven.

There won't be any TV because who's going to make the programmes if nobody is working? And why would you have to learn anything from books or videos when God can just implant all the knowledge of the Universe in you instantly?

No need to clean things. Heaven is not going to get dusty because most dust is made of dead skin cells. Your skin isn't going to die in Heaven is it?

No need to go shopping – owning material goods is sure to create envy and competitiveness, which are all bad things.

No sport, because that is way too competitive – it implies winners and losers, and surely there are no losers in Heaven.

No art, because if you painted a picture what if it wasn't very good? Who would tell you? Nobody is going to hurt your feelings when you're in Heaven, because again that's emotional pain, even if it's on a small scale.

Music? Same as art. And where would be the challenge in composing a new piano concerto? You can do it instantly, because the frustration that musicians go through when they are composing won't be there.

There won't be any research into the history of the past because God knows everything and he can just tell you everything that ever happened.

No need for science or technology. God made all the laws of science, so he knows all the answers. If you want something it will just be provided for you, no questions asked.

Life will be very, very, very, very easy.

God's Purpose.

And what is God going to do? He created man, destroyed most of them in the Flood, had his son tortured and killed, and pretty soon (so the Fundies tell us) he'll be sending him down again for a second time, and finally destroying the whole of the Earth, saving only the born-again Christians. The rest, about 90% of the population, will be sent 'down there' to be tortured and burned for all eternity.

So what will God's purpose be after the second coming? Good question, because it's clear that he will no longer have a purpose.

Unless... he gets bored and starts the whole thing off again. Time to create another Universe, make more toy people, and play with them until they misbehave and he has to kill them.

Doesn't this all sound a bit... lame?

Heaven is a place where you go to do nothing. You'll just be a spaced-out hippy looking at waterfalls and playing with rabbits. You won't have to try hard to do *anything*. Everything will be easy. Unlike on Earth, where if you make something or do something you feel a sense of achievement, you will get none of that in Heaven.

You're going to be bored out of your tiny little mind for all eternity. And that's a long, long time. At least Hell has decent night life.

On the other hand, if you think that Heaven isn't there, and that your purpose in life is *not* to try to get there, you can make your own decisions about your purpose in life. If you want to be an explorer, or an artist, or a teacher, you can do it, and know that the rewards will be the day-to-day achievements that come from being alive. You can put your all into living, and not have to worry about being 'good enough' to get to Heaven.

If you think you're going to win eternal peace after you die, try sitting in a room looking out of the window doing nothing else for a day or two. Now do that for a week. Now try a year. Keep doing it for a *billion* years. That's eternal peace. It's also known as eternal boredom.

There is no big prize at the end of life. Your reward is being happy for as long as you're alive on Earth, knowing that you've got one life and no second chances after you die. If you want to live your life just so that you can get to a non-existent place you think will welcome you after you die, you're going to waste a big part of every single day you have on this planet. You may as well just sit down with your Bible and do nothing but praise the big invisible man in the sky.

Even if Heaven does exist, and as an atheist I'm here to tell you it doesn't, you won't have any purpose when you get there. You'll be stuck there for all eternity doing nothing but 'happy things'. And the only people I know who are happy 24 hours a day are the people they put in nice, safe, padded cells.

Atheist Heaven.

Who put that sub-title there? Atheist Heaven? Everyone knows that atheists don't go to Heaven. We don't even believe it exists. But for Christians, just the *thought* of going to Heaven when they die keeps them happy and fulfilled. How can atheism match that feeling? You know the one, the feeling that gives the faithful that look of smug satisfaction and total self-righteousness.

The good news is that atheists can find comfort in the fact that Heaven does *not* exist. Even though we don't get to meet God, we don't get our own cloud and some nice wings to float around on, and we don't get a new white toga every day, there are several advantages, some great things that having no Heaven can do for us.

Number one, and this is the most important of all: once you're dead and gone you won't have to listen to Gospel music ever again. All that Hallelujah stuff will be over and done with for good when you die. No more singing.

Second thing. When you die you won't have to listen to Christians going on and on about God any more. Obviously if you went to Heaven they'd be talking about him all the time. God did this, God did that, ooh look at how marvellous God is, let's praise him for another hour or five shall we? And he's always there (omnipresent, remember) so you'll get no privacy. For atheists, no going to Heaven so none of that. As soon as your heart stops, all that Christian crap will stop too.

My personal philosophy about death is this. Death is like the quiet moment just after you do a loud fart in the elevator. For a split second time stops. Everything goes quiet. That's how quiet death is.

Another advantage: you won't be living in a place where smoking, drinking and sex are banned. Do you *really* want to go to a place like that? No fatty foods, no unhealthy diet. Do you know what that means? No pizza!

And no Jack Daniel's, no vodka. No beer. How could there be a Hell worse than a place with no beer?

Someone like God would never let you drink so much beer that it was leaking out of your ears, before you stagger home and spew it all up in the toilet. God works in mysterious ways, but the Bible never mentions the mysterious carpet stains which appear after a night out on the ale, so obviously this is not going to happen in Heaven.

Once again, the good news is, you can do all that on Earth as much as you like, and the only punishment will be liver failure. And marriage breakdown. And the occasional weird substance on your shirt that won't come out, even with industrial bleach.

But that's your choice. No one will stick a meat hook up your back end and lower you over hot coals for a million years just for having a few drinks now and again.

It's the little things that are important.

Little things, tiny things that Christians still call sins, they won't matter to atheists either. Remember that if Heaven doesn't exist, then neither does Hell. Which is just as well…

Just because you didn't apologise to Jesus when some idiot trod on your foot and you called him a clumsy bastard, you don't have to be afraid that you're going to burn in Hell for that.

If your wife invites her friends round, just when you want to watch the late-night football, you won't be tortured for a billion years just because you called her a thoughtless bitch when she wasn't there, or was out of earshot. It won't matter. You won't need to be forgiven if she wasn't listening.

If you call your wife a thoughtless bitch when she *is* listening, you *will* need to be forgiven, but you won't need God's forgiveness – it will be much, much worse than that.

But you can still get revenge on her, by putting a light sprinkling of salt, or maybe some ground-up laxatives, on all the food she's bought for the girls to eat while they watch Titanic for the 50th time. It might be naughty, but you'll get away with it. There is no Satan to turn up the gas burners an extra degree.

All you people who work in McDonald's, don't worry if you spit in a customer's cheeseburger when they shout at you for getting their order wrong. Even though you shouldn't do it, nobody will punish you for it and you don't *need* to pray for forgiveness. After all, working at McDonald's is punishment enough.

Men, if you walk down the street and stare at some woman's breasts, that's okay. It's not a problem. If nobody sees you, nobody minds, and you can have all the lustful thoughts you want. It's not a sin, it's human nature. No praying to God to forgive you for worshipping the breasts.

Don't forget, it says in the Bible do not worship false gods. It says nothing about worshipping false breasts. Nothing. I've checked.

Women (let's be fair and equal here), if you 'let your fingers do the walking' when you're looking at a picture of Tom Cruise (or even Penelope Cruz), don't worry, just give them a good wash afterwards and no need to pray because you won't be going to Hell either. You don't even need to worry about it. Most women do it... or at least all the ones in my, er, friend's video collection. It's not a sin. Apparently.

Gay people, you can have as much fun as you want, and nobody will punish you for it. Unless you go to one of those clubs with the whips and the leather and... I wouldn't know about that, obviously.

It's all natural.

Here are some really important points. If you thought that global warming was God's punishment or the second coming of Jesus, you don't need to worry. It's just the melting of the polar ice caps and it's a man-made thing. By the time all the Christians have worked that out, it will be too late to stop it anyway. We're all going to drown. So don't worry about it.

Two pieces of advice on that: buy an umbrella and move away from the coast, because it's going to get a bit wet in the next few years. Or it could get hot. Or maybe both. Global warming is a bit weird that way.

Number two: tsunamis and earthquakes are natural. They are not brought on by God. So move away from the damned earthquake zones if you know what's good for you. The San Andreas Fault is due for a big one any time now, so *move*. It's not the final judgement. It's not Jesus come back to destroy the Earth and take all his friends away with him. It's tectonic plates, moving around, and you really don't want to get in the way.

Finally: if you're a bit worried that although you believe in God you might have the wrong god... don't worry, all gods are the same. They aren't there. And in times of crisis they can't help you.

So if God isn't there, what can you do instead of pray? Well, instead of just sitting there with your hands together or up in the air, try this. Lean forward, stand up, walk out of the door, and get out there and *do something* with your life.

You only get one life and there is no afterlife. Even though you're not going to burn in Hell, you won't get rewarded in Heaven either. So make the most of your life. It's all you've got, but you can do a lot with it if you try.

Just be happy – if you don't, you've only got yourself to blame.

Except if you have cancer of course. That's not your fault.

5

Intelligent Design = Creationism

The wolf in sheep's clothing.

The people who support Intelligent Design want you to know that a supernatural designer created everyone, and that the 'science' of Intelligent Design isn't Creationism or Christianity in disguise.

However, you can't teach religion in schools, so ID is put forward as a sort of non-religious scientific theory, an alternative to Big Bang Theory and Evolution Theory.

Basically, the story is this: some things are so complex that they could never have evolved, so they *must* have been designed. And if *some* things are designed by a supernatural being, everything else in the natural world must have been designed too.

There's a problem with that, and it's this:

If it's *obvious* that a designer made the Universe, isn't it also obvious that there must have been more than one designer?

In fact there must have been a whole team of designers – thousands, millions, all working in their individual departments. Because you don't just have designers, you need manufacturers too. Look at one of the examples that supporters of Intelligent Design give:

> If you found a computer in a forest you would *know* that
> it had been designed.

Obviously, that's right. But you'd also know that hundreds of people had developed that design over a period of many years. There is no way you'd ever believe that one person had designed and built that computer. It's just too complex for one person to build, particularly if you make the assumption that it was built 'from nothing', ie not simply from a bag of parts, but from the raw materials found in the ground.

Intelligent Design = Creationism

Another example that Intelligent Design people like to give is a watch. Let's assume we're talking about watches in the days when one person could actually make a watch. A skilled craftsman, the watch maker, would spend weeks putting together intricate mechanisms, making valuable watches for rich clients.

But he didn't do it all himself. Watch makers don't make all the watch parts. He didn't dig up the copper and zinc ores, melt them down and mix them to make brass. He didn't mine the gold and silver for the case. He didn't dig up diamonds and cut them to decorate the watch. He didn't heat sand and mould it to make glass for the face, or mix the ink for the numbers on the dial. And someone else made all his tools – his tweezers, his magnifying glass, everything.

If it's a modern watch, who made the battery? Who invented the technology for the battery? Who raised the cow and killed it to get leather for the strap?

Watches and computers both need teams of people to create them. According to Intelligent Design, some things are so complex they *must* have been designed. If that's the case, why would anyone assume that something even more complex, like a plant or an animal, would not need a huge *team* of designers and manufacturers to build it? How could you even think there could only be one designer?

Intelligent Design supporters have *never* suggested there might be a team of designers all busy in their inter-galactic workshops. Because that would sound just a little too much like Santa and his elves, and that would be silly wouldn't it?

So why do Intelligent Design supporters only ever talk of one designer?

The answer to that is: Intelligent Design is not science, it's religion, pure and simple. And that religion is Christianity. There are no Muslim Intelligent Design advocates. There are no Buddhist Intelligent Design lecturers. There are no Jewish Intelligent Design organisations.

There are no suggestions of multiple designers because Christianity has only one designer, and that's the Christian God. Christians invented Intelligent Design for one reason only: to sneak Christianity into schools through the back door and pretend that it's a scientific alternative to evolution.

But even complex things like watches and computers have evolved. We didn't go straight from sun-dials to super-accurate quartz watches. And we didn't go from the abacus to high-powered wi-fi laptops in one giant leap either.

Innovations are developed over time, building on top of previous models, taking the best ideas and adding new ones. Improvements are made each time, and the design evolves. Some inventions reach a dead-end and become extinct, like Betamax tapes. Others keep evolving into more complex models, like new generations of PCs.

Like the Neanderthals and Homo sapiens, we now have Windows PCs and Apple Macs – two separate 'species' that evolved from the same common ancestor. And of course the chips inside, the 'brains' of those computers, keep evolving year after year.

So how could you possibly look at something as complex as a human and think 'one designer made that from scratch, instantly, totally out of the nothing, with no blueprint, no earlier models, nothing else to go on'? Isn't it more logical to think that life evolved, slowly, over hundreds of millions of years, using natural selection?

If Intelligent Design is going to be taught as science, let's just assume that the only sensible position is that there are many more designers than just one. And that's not going to happen because don't forget, it's Christian Creationism here, not any kind of independent scientific theory.

Better still, just scrap Intelligent Design. Then we can keep religion completely separate from *real* science.

God Almighty's Genesis Diary – Day 1

Day 1 – Monday

8:00 am

Woke up bright and early, ready to start work. Bit dark outside. When I tried to turn the light on to get dressed, I realised I hadn't actually made light yet.

Damn.

I hate Mondays, I'm always so forgetful. And it's not as if I've had anything else to do lately is it? In fact it was so dark that I put my underpants on inside out. First day at work and the omnipotence is not quite firing on all cylinders, but I'm sure I'll get into the swing of things when I've woken up properly.

8:30 am

Things got worse when I realised that breakfast was out of the question – no chance of the light coming on in the fridge, not until I'd made a start. Then again…

Let there be breakfast!

Actually, I'm not all that hungry. Can I cancel that? I must remember not to mention that my first act of Creation was forming a bowl of corn flakes out of the nothingness. It doesn't sound very impressive does it? Still, who's to know? There's only me here.

Nothing much on TV this morning.

9:15 am

Bit of a late start, but here we go.

Let there be light!

9:20 am

Something's wrong. I think the bulb's gone. Wait a minute, can I have light if there's nothing to actually light up?

Ah, right. Heaven first, Earth second and then the light. Look, this is the first time I've done this so I'm learning as I go along. Don't blame me if the Earth turns out flat, or has the stars spinning around it, or something equally freaky.

These flat-pack self-build Universes are a bit of a nightmare. And as expected, no instructions in Aramaic.

9:45 am

Omnipotence isn't all it's cracked up to be. I assume I have the power, it's knowing how to get it working. Still no light, but at least I can see now. Apparently seeing in the dark is one of my powers. Well thanks for letting me know.

Hmm, that Earth thing looks a bit formless. But not too bad for a first attempt I suppose. I'll have to look into it later, see if I can't spruce it up a bit. That bloody darkness is everywhere though. It's really getting on my tits. I'm going to have to sort it out. Back soon.

10:30 am

I knew I shouldn't have gone out in just my slippers.

There's water everywhere, and I stepped right in it. If I'd known it was there I could have walked over it but oh no, in we go, right up to the ankles. If the rest of the week is going to be like this I'm just going to end up not bothering.

Decided to have the rest of the morning off. The electric blanket was still on so I had a bit of a nap. Cat hairs on the bed again.

12:30 pm

I'm ready. I'm going for it.
Let there be light!
Bugger me, it worked. That was good, even though I say it myself.
Who's the Father? I'm the Father, that's who!

12:50 pm

Right, let's get this sodding darkness out of the way. Darkness, get thee to that side! Light, over this way. Now if they'll just stay there I can finally get something done.

1:30 pm

Organisation, that's what this job needs! I really should start giving these things names, before I start to lose track. With all the things I've got planned for the rest of the week, I need to stay on top of my game.

Obviously I'll call the light Day. I mean, it just fits doesn't it? Daylight – day, light. Easy. Although... Sunlight. I could call it Sun. No, Day will do. But I like that word. Sun. Sun, Sun, Sun. I'll call something else Sun.

Okay, the dark. I know what I'd *like* to call it. Shitty Black Stuff That Keeps Crawling All Over Creation. Doesn't really trip off the tongue though does it? What about Night? Neat? Note? Newt?

Tea break!

2:15 pm

Sod it, Night will do. Go with the first idea to save work. Good plan. Now I need a couple more. Evening and morning is where the night stops and the day starts, or is it the other way round? I'll write it down and work it out later.

Oh who cares? They're just names. Nobody will question me, so it's no big deal.

3:15pm

Look at the time! I spend 20 minutes making light and then two whole hours finding names for all the other stuff! All this admin crap annoys the Hell out of me. Paperwork – it's just not why I took this job. Practical and down to earth, that's the kind of God I am. That's the reason I'm doing this job in the first place. But typing, filing, copying... can't I just say, 'Let the paperwork be done'? If only.

4:00 pm

I'm calling it a day.
You're a day!
Just my little joke. And anyway I've used that name already.

7

Bible Prophecies Prove Nothing

Proving a myth.

Since I started talking and writing about atheism, several Christians felt the need to contact me to say, 'Look, the Bible is the truth and the word of God. You shouldn't be doubting that.'

And that's fine, I acknowledge those views because Christians believe in one thing, I believe in another, and although they're wrong and I'm right(!), I have to accept that they believe in God and Jesus.

But like Zeus, like Ra, like Odin, the God of the Bible does not exist. The Bible is simply a set of myths and legends and stories. And that's the same for the Qur'an, the Bhagavad Gita, and all the other supposedly divinely inspired books that have been written, *by humans*, over the course of history. They are *all* myths and legends, and although they are interesting from a historical or an intellectual point of view, they aren't facts.

And yet some Christians, after claiming that the Bible is true, will add, 'We can *prove* the Bible is true.' And there they enter into a discussion which they cannot hope to win.

Of course proof that everything (or even *something*) in the Bible is true would be wonderful. For a start it would completely destroy the arguments of all atheists. If you can prove it, then there's no argument. Atheists would be wrong, Christians would be right, if only the contents of the Bible could be proven beyond reasonable doubt.

Predicting the past.

The main kind of proof you will hear quoted is 'Biblical prophecy'. The Old Testament has hundreds of prophecies, predicting all manner of events, including the coming of the Messiah.

Some of these prophecies are vague, some are quite specific, but regardless of that, if they came true, it *must* mean that the Bible is the word of God because he would know the future, right?

So I asked a few Christians how they knew the Bible prophecies came true, and I got a great answer:

> We known the Bible prophecies came true because it says so in the Bible.

You can see my problem with this. It's like saying that there are prophecies in the first book of the Harry Potter series. Then when the other books in the series are published, amazingly enough all the prophecies in Harry Potter's 'Old Testament' came true. Amazing! Who could have expected that?

And because what happens in the new Harry Potter books ties in so closely with the prophecies in the older books, are we supposed to believe that Harry Potter books are true?

Of course not.

But isn't this what we are expected to believe with the Bible? A series of writers in ancient times put together the prophecies in the Old Testament. Then later on, another set of people, who already knew about those prophecies, wrote that they had been fulfilled.

Would it not be so tempting to say, 'Okay, here's a prophecy. It says the Messiah will ride into a city on an ass. Cool, we'll write that the Messiah rode into the city on an ass, because if we write that he walked in, or came in on a camel, people are going to say he's not the Messiah.'

But it's worse than that, because even if you don't believe that they twisted the truth to make it look like certain things happened, well, they still made a bad job of telling the story anyway, because the Bible doesn't just try to confirm its own prophecies, it contradicts itself while it's doing it.

Here's an example. According to the Bible, the Messiah must be the physical descendant of David. But how could that be the case if he is the son of God and not the son of Joseph? Even aside from that, there are two completely different family trees for Jesus in the Bible.

And I do mean completely.

From David to Jesus, there are dozens of names, but hardly any of the names match when you look at the list in Matthew and the list in Luke. Take a look – Matthew 1 and Luke 3 just don't match up.

Even the name of Jesus' grandfather is different, and you'd have thought they'd get the name of Joseph's Dad right wouldn't you?

There are also prophecies that Jesus is supposed to have made, and which the Bible says came true, but when you look at them it gets the story all mixed up.

Things as simple as saying that the cock shall not crow until Peter has denied Jesus three times. Well, in one of the gospels Peter only denies him *once* before the cock crows, not three times. So the biblical writers are a little confused there.

Isn't the Bible the inspired word of God? If so, why did God tell John one thing about Jesus (the cock crowing three times) and then tell Mark another (it only crowed once). Either God is lying to one of them, or John and Mark didn't swap enough notes and they made the mistakes themselves. Or, and this is a possibility, they made it all up.

There are also prophecies that *we didn't even know about* but that the Bible says came true.

The Bible says that during Jesus' crucifixion, the soldiers didn't break his legs because he was already dead. John 19:36 claims that this fulfilled a prophecy: 'Not a bone of him shall be broken.'

But there is no such prophecy. How you can use this to prove that a prophecy came true, when the prophecy doesn't exist?

Jesus himself said that Moses spoke about him, which of course would have been a form of prophecy: 'For had ye believed Moses, ye would have believed me; for he wrote of me' (John 5:46). Sorry, Moses makes no mention of Jesus, so this is another prophecy that didn't actually happen.

There are quite a few cases like this, and Christians have told me that this is probably because these are prophecies not recorded in the Bible.

So now we are asked to believe that the *proof* in the Bible is the 'fact' that an *unknown* prophecy, which has no record of ever being made at all, came true. This is proof that the Bible writers aren't making it up? Give me a break.

There's another group of prophecies: ones that didn't come true at all. So we got them on that, then – atheism wins!

Bible Prophecies Prove Nothing   47

But oh no, Christians say that these prophecies, ones which the Bible doesn't say came true, are prophecies for the future, and they *will* come true one day.

What can I say? You really can't argue a case when Christianity gives you twisted logic like that. So all the prophecies which came true are proof, and all the ones which didn't come true simply haven't happened yet, so that gives the Bible a 100% record. Okaaaay…

It's not proof if you can't prove it.

The problem with the so-called 'proof' in the Bible is that there is no objective, third-party corroboration for *any* of the stories in the New Testament.

But this was a long time ago. Surely we could not expect evidence to survive for 2000 years? If Jesus had lived among the ancient tribes of the Americas, that may have been so (and the Mormons have their own story about that!). In many parts of the world there are no written records at all, and we have to piece together fragments of history, giving a very incomplete picture.

Yet the story of Jesus is set in a particular time and a particular place. The Roman Empire in the first century AD is the most historically documented and recorded period in the entire span of ancient history, bar none. It was the time of the first Roman emperors: Augustus, Tiberius, Caligula, Claudius, Nero. There are *masses* of documents from this period. The Romans wrote histories about *all* the major events of the time.

Judea was a Roman province, under Roman control, so if there was a major disturbance like, oh, the coming of the Jewish Messiah, someone would have written about it.

But nobody did.

Well perhaps the documents were lost? We've lost a lot of Roman writings over the years of course. Civilisations come and go, wars destroy whole cities, and documents burn or decompose very easily.

On the other hand, many documents do survive, and you have to think about why some of those ancient writings still exist today. By copying and re-copying over the centuries, usually by religious people, who were generally the only ones who could read and write, ancient texts have been made available to us. These people thought that the lives of the ancient Romans were great enough to remember and so copied and preserved their histories.

So if Jesus had been mentioned anywhere by a contemporary writer, wouldn't that writing have been the single most important document for Christian scholars to keep alive, to copy and re-copy? And yet such a document does not exist.

In fact there are *no* documents from writers who were alive in the dates that Jesus Christ is supposed to have lived, which also mention Jesus. None.

No one saw Jesus, no one knew the story of Jesus.

If there is no other mention of Jesus other than in the Bible, how can that be proof that the Bible is true?

So basically we have:

- Prophecies in the Old Testament, which the New Testament (still the same book, the Bible) says came true, written by people who knew that if the stories didn't match, nobody would believe them.

- Prophecies that the Bible says came true, but they came true in several different ways, at least one of which cannot be true because it invalidates the other (like the 2 family trees of Jesus)

- Prophecies that Jesus made, and which came true, but again, you wouldn't write a story where the start didn't match the end.

- Prophecies that Jesus made but he messed up because it didn't quite work out that way, like the cock crowing. That's just showing that two different gospel writers didn't share notes well enough.

- Prophecies that the Bible says came true, but when you look into it the original prophecy is nowhere to be seen. I could tell you that in ancient times there was a prophecy that I would write this book, but that the prophecy was not written anywhere. An lo! The book is written! In other words, the prophecy came true but someone forget to mention that it wasn't a prophecy at all.

- Prophecies that didn't come true, but because they didn't, well, that's just because they are still prophecies and they will happen in the future. How do you argue with that kind of logic?

- And finally, we have no unbiased reports of *any* of these things happening. No eye witnesses, no documents that aren't in the Bible, despite this being the most well documented period in ancient history.

So all I have to say to Christians is: where is your proof?

There is no proof except what's in the Bible, and the argument that the Bible is proof that the Bible is true is a circular argument and it just doesn't hold water.

Proof is not something to be taken lightly. On my list of 'quotes that atheists love to use' is the following gem from Carl Sagan, which you will recognise I'm sure:

Extraordinary claims require extraordinary evidence.

There is *no* extraordinary evidence that the Bible is anything other than a series of stories, myths and legends which, like all folklore, changed and evolved over the centuries. In that respect the Bible is as true as the legends of Robin Hood or King Arthur, or the myths of the Greek or Norse gods.

8

What Are You? Some Kind of Atheist?

Definitions.

Evangelical Christians, the hard-line, in-your-face Fundamentalists of Christianity, have a hard time with atheists. It really doesn't enter into their minds that actually, no, an atheist does not believe in God. What I hear, and I hear this a lot, is that atheists *reject* God. Which is really saying that we believe in an invisible man in the sky, but that we've decided to simply raise the middle finger – we know he's there but we don't want to have anything to do with him.

This Christian definition of atheism is utterly wrong.

Atheists do not believe in God. Period. How can a person reject something they don't even believe exists? By the same definition, atheists would reject Santa, or the tooth fairy. Clearly, an absence of belief is not the same as a rejection of something believed to exist.

This corruption of terms, and the deliberate misunderstanding of people's beliefs (or absence of them) seems to be a key 'weapon' of Evangelicals, and it's a pretty weak weapon at that. But they use it anyway, and its purpose, like all forms of religion, is not to unite people but to divide them, to separate the 'true' Christians (and of course the Evangelicals think that they are the only ones worthy of the name 'Christian') from the rest.

Personally I think that if you say you're a Christian, that's what you are. If you say you're an atheist, you're an atheist. But there are people who will try to say, 'Well, technically, you're not an atheist, you're an agnostic,' or, 'Just because someone goes to church and prays, that doesn't make them a Christian'. The people who quibble about semantics in this way are simply trying to steer the conversation into trivial areas which really don't warrant any heated discussions at all.

So why am I writing this chapter if definitions are unimportant? Well, if you're an atheist you need to know what you're up against. You and I might not want to discuss them, but they'll be thrown in our faces anyway.

If someone tells you point blank that you're not what you say you are, or that your definition of an atheist, an agnostic, or a Christian is not the same as theirs, it's useful to be able to understand what is going on, that the person who says these things just wants a chance to prove you wrong. There is no merit in any of these arguments, and they can be dismissed very easily.

Atheist or agnostic?

To understand what 'atheism' means, you first need to know that it is actually a two-part word. Those two parts are 'a' and 'theism'.

'Theism' is defined as 'belief in the existence of a god or gods, especially belief in a personal God as creator and ruler of the world'. Or, to shorten and that, we might say that theism is 'belief in God'. This means that all Christians are theists, all Muslims are theists, as are all Jews, Hindus, Sikhs, and followers of many other religions.

The 'a' in 'atheism' means 'without', so atheism is 'without belief in God'. An atheist simply has no belief in God. In itself this is not a belief. If you'd never heard of God at all, you certainly wouldn't believe in him, but you could not say that you believed he did not exist. Do you believe that the god Wonatui-Banaka does not exist? No, because you've never heard of him (I just made him up).

Even if you'd heard of God, you might not have given him much thought. You'd be an atheist in all these cases. Absence of belief is not a belief in itself.

Everyone in the world is either a theist or an atheist. You either believe in a god (and that could be any god) or you don't. And this is where we get into troubled waters, because there is another word that we need to throw into the discussion: agnostic.

This is another two-part word. Once again 'a' means 'without', but combined with 'gnosis', meaning 'knowledge', we have 'without knowledge'.

An agnostic is someone who believes that it is impossible to know whether there is a God. From that very simple definition, the pettiest arguments and squabbles can arise, because technically *everyone* is agnostic. Without proof, nothing is 'known' with 100% certainty. God is invisible, but that could also be because he isn't there, so we cannot *know* he exists. Some people *believe* he does, some do not.

Even with our fictional god, Wonatui-Banaka, the correct position would still be agnosticism. After all, there may be many gods, and one of them might be called Wonatui-Banaka. You cannot prove he isn't out there somewhere.

But 'belief' and 'knowledge' are entirely separate. A Christian can believe in God, but may still recognise that he cannot know for certain that God exists. That makes him agnostic. And yet an atheist, who has no belief in God, may concede that there is a tiny, remote chance, but that we cannot know for certain. And again, that makes him agnostic. You can be religious *and* agnostic, or atheist *and* agnostic. The two are not mutually exclusive.

In fact the only sensible statement, in my opinion, is that the word 'agnostic' is meaningless when used alone. Unless you say that you are atheist-agnostic, or Christian-agnostic, for example, nobody knows which side of the fence you come down on. Agnosticism is about knowledge, not about belief.

The fact that we are *all* agnostic should be obvious. Of course we cannot know with 100% certainty that God exists, or that he does not. We couldn't prove the negative because we would need perfect knowledge of the entire Universe, and even then, since God is a supernatural concept, we are looking for something which might be beyond our ability to detect it.

God himself could prove that he exists, simply by waving from the sky, and speaking to us in a booming voice, but so far this hasn't happened. We are all therefore agnostic.

Don't call me that!

People who call themselves agnostic don't like to be called atheists, though usually that is exactly what they are – they don't believe in God, but they may be open to change if the right proof comes along. Most atheists think that proof will *never* come along, but that is a separate issue.

What Are You? Some Kind of Atheist?

Similarly, many atheists don't like to be called agnostic, even though technically that is the sensible position – if you cannot *prove* that God does not exist, then there is a chance (however laughable you may find that notion) that he might.

Of course Christians don't like being called agnostic either! Try telling an Evangelical Christian that he can't prove that God exists – I dare you!

What do we have so far? Let's summarise:

- Theism is the belief that a God or God exists
- Atheism is the absence of such a belief
- Agnosticism is the recognition that we cannot know for certain which of the two, theism or atheism, is correct.
- A person can be theist-agnostic or atheist-agnostic.

Since we are all agnostic anyway, why not dispense with the word completely? Some agnostics genuinely do not know what to believe, and if pressed could not tell you whether or not they believe in God. If *really* pressed, in my experience they will almost always give you an answer which suggests that they are atheists, but will vigorously object to such a description of themselves.

It may be more useful to think of this in terms of a person's belief in 'luck'. Even some strong atheists are superstitious, but could not tell you if they truly believe that the strange coincidences we sometimes experience are luck or mere chance. Most people would probably be (in this sense of the word) agnostic about the existence of 'luck'.[1]

---

[1] To further muddy the waters, consider this statement: my car is blue. Do you believe that is true or false? Are you an atheist (to borrow the word for the sake of this explanation) about my car's blueness? Most people would have no opinion either way – they simply don't have enough knowledge on which to base an opinion. In this case you would appear to be agnostic, a self-contained agnostic, neither atheist-agnostic nor theist-agnostic. I therefore disprove my own argument! Or do I? No. Theism is belief in a god or gods. Atheism is an absence of that belief. If you do not explicitly *believe* that my car is blue, you have an absence of belief. You do not have to *believe* that my car is *not* blue to be atheistic about the subject. Recall the introduction to this book: atheists do not have to *believe* that there is no god (although some do). They simply lack belief that there is. So my argument stands: you are either a theist or an atheist, and we are *all* agnostic. See why this subject stirs the opinions of so many people?

You can see that arguments can easily arise over these fairly simple terms. And don't worry, it gets much better than this! For one thing, we can divide atheists into two groups: strong atheists and weak atheists.

Strong or weak?

The terms 'strong atheist' and 'weak atheist' are in no way meant to be derogatory. A 'strong' atheist is someone who positively asserts that there is no God. As you might expect, I consider myself a strong atheist. A 'weak' atheist is someone who basically has very little interest in talking about the subject at all, and simply has no belief in God.

Most atheists are weak atheists. If you don't believe in God, there is actually very little benefit to be had from talking about it – after all, that's what religious people do, and who would want to get into discussions about religion when it does not interest them in the slightest?

By contrast there are no 'strong' Christians or 'weak' Christians (though there are certainly very vocal ones!), because Christianity *demands* the assertion of faith in God and Jesus Christ. To be a Christian there are certain things you must do, and by definition if you have little interest in Christianity, never go to church, in fact do nothing religious at all, you can't really call yourself a Christian.

To further add to the confusion, Evangelical Christians will tell you that they are the only 'true' Christians, and that going to church is not enough. Praying to God is not enough. *Saying* that you are a Christian does not make you a Christian, so say the Evangelicals. This is a far bigger discussion, and I will cover it in a later chapter.

There are many misconceptions about atheists and atheism. I will try to cover a few of them here.

Is atheism a belief?

Most atheists will say no, that by definition atheism is simply the *absence* of belief in God. Certainly for all weak atheists it is not a belief. However, I take a slightly more controversial view. Since I am a strong atheist, or perhaps I can be better described as an *active* atheist, I *do* believe something: I believe there is no God.

The first time I said that on my YouTube video blog I was beset by a horde of angry comments, saying that I had betrayed atheism and had no right to say that atheism was a belief. But I never said that. All I said was that I believe there is no God. Isn't that just the same as saying that I don't believe there *is* a God? Reactions were still mixed. Some went as far as to give detailed explanations about why atheism is absolutely not a belief. It seems that even atheists fall into this trap of discussing whether or not atheism is a belief.

Unlike religion, atheism is certainly not a belief *system*. You don't have to actually *do* anything to be an atheist. If I stopped talking or writing about atheism, I would still be an atheist. The fact that I believe there is no God simply means that I've heard people talking about God, I've read information, looked into the subject closely, and based on all the (lack of) evidence, I have concluded that there is no God. That's what I believe is the right position to take.

With respect to Hinduism, about which I profess to know much less than I do about Christianity, I may be better described as a weak atheist. But since I don't believe in the supernatural at all, and all gods are by definition supernatural, I might be coaxed into saying that I believe that the Hindu gods do not exist.

If you agree or disagree with that analysis, does it really matter? These are just semantics. Even if atheism was a belief *system*, why do we even need to discuss this? Christians will point and say, 'Aha! Atheism is just as much a belief as Christianity.' Although it's not, would it matter if it was? Would it change the fact that atheists don't believe in an invisible supernatural being?

The common denominator is that all atheists have no belief in a god or gods. We *all* have that in common.

There are more important discussions to be had than this, and the purpose of this article is to make it clear that this is perhaps the *least* important topic you could ever hope to find based around the subject of atheism.

Does atheism require faith?

No. Faith is slightly different. One of the definitions of faith is 'belief that does not rest on logical proof or material evidence'. Many atheists justify their absence of belief in God by pointing to the material evidence of the natural world, which science describes for us to the best of its ability. The fact that science describes the natural world, and the natural world correspondingly shows evidence that science is correct, is not faith. Christians cannot 'go and check' that God exists. Atheists *can* 'go and check' that science is correct, because science is based entirely on evidence. It is testable. It is reproducible. There is data. There are observations which can be made to verify that data.

Christianity, meanwhile, is based almost entirely on faith – believing in something for which sufficient evidence does not exist.

Is atheism a religion?

No. This is the silliest question of all. You won't find atheists praying to gravity, or to evolution. Nobody wakes up and gives thanks to science for inventing the digital alarm clock or the pop-up toaster.

Atheists don't have to believe in anything in particular, although most atheists share the belief that science has explanations for most of what we see around us, and has *proof* for its assertions. But even if you don't believe in evolution you can still be an atheist. Acceptance of Big Bang Theory is also not a requirement. You won't have to promise to devote your life to atheism, and there is no reward after death for your absence of belief in a god or gods.

Some will argue that atheists adhere to pseudo-religious dogma just as much as any religious person. Charles Darwin's *The Origin of Species* is usually mentioned. But acceptance of the contents of this book is completely separate from atheism. Atheists do not swear oaths on it, nor do they even have to accept that it contains a proven theory. However, most atheists *do* accept it because there is *evidence* that it is correct. Atheism is simply not a religion by any recognisable definition of the word.

Does it take as much faith to be an atheist as it does to be a Christian?

Why would it? We are all born atheists. How difficult was it to be an atheist infant, before outside influences started to try to persuade us that God was real? Let's compare religion with atheism and see what takes a greater amount of faith.

1. Belief in a world which is based on natural laws, which happens to be consistent with what we see around us

2. Belief in a giant invisible man in the sky, who is all powerful, who made the entire Universe in six days, who can read our minds (that's everybody, all at once), knows the future, can disrupt the fabric of time and space to perform miracles, and who has prepared a special place for non-believers where they will burn forever as a punishment.

Surely it's obvious that the second position requires far more faith than the first, atheistic, viewpoint.

Discussions about semantics are ultimately futile, because in the end people are individuals. If you want to argue with someone who calls himself agnostic, be my guest, but you would be better served by simply asking him what he means, what his views are on religion, and then abandoning any perceived labels altogether. Then you can move on to far more interesting topics.

Spend no time wondering about these definitions, because one word, be it atheist, theist, agnostic, Christian, Muslim or any other simplistic term, cannot describe the complexity of a unique individual with many diverse opinions and, yes, beliefs.

9

'True' Christians

Lies, damned lies and Evangelists.

We're back on definitions again, but this time the definitions that Christians give themselves. Why would this be important to atheists? The definition itself is not important, but the division and downright hatred that these definitions cause are obvious. Religions of all descriptions are touted as welcoming, inclusive and uniting... except if you don't happen to be a member, that is.

The blogging scene on YouTube is often interrupted by isolated members who put out videos which for whatever reason become the centre of attention for a short while. Such a video turned up from an American Christian woman, and the atheists leapt on it with great glee.

In it, the woman, a proclaimed Evangelical Christian (I'll call her EC from now on), said that she had seen a poll which claimed that 84% of people in America are Christians. She, however, maintained that the actual figure was different. Not just slightly different. *Significantly* different.

EC wanted us to know that, in fact, only 7% of Americans are actually Christians. That's not a misprint, that is *seven per cent*.

Her justification?

In her words, only 33% of Americans go to church, only 2 out of 3 of those really 'get it' and only a few of those are actually Evangelists. This left only a small 7% of Americans, the only *true* Christians.

True Christians. This is a phrase you may not have heard before, but now that you know it you will find it everywhere. Apparently only Evangelists are 'true' Christians. All the other Christians will be going straight to Hell, probably on the same bus as the Muslims, Jews and atheists.

Seriously. That is what Evangelicals believe.

Now I'm an atheist, but I know people who believe in Jesus and don't go to church. These people would be immensely offended if they heard someone claiming that, because they weren't Evangelists, they weren't really Christians.

EC felt that as her 7% was in the minority, they were being persecuted. According to her, atheists outnumber Christians. Yes that's right, she believes there are more atheists than Christians – *in America*.

The truth of the matter is that it's not the Evangelists (the so-called 'true' Christians) who are being persecuted, it is the ordinary Christians who are happy to go about their lives and just *be Christians*, the 77% that EC maintains are not really Christians at all because they don't go to church, or they 'don't get it' (this concept was never explained), or even if they do, they aren't Evangelists.

My video response pointed out, in no uncertain terms, that an immediate reality check was needed. The *Pope* isn't an Evangelist, he's a Catholic. Was she seriously asking everyone to accept that the Pope and all the *billion* Catholics in the world aren't actually Christians? So the Pope is what? An atheist? I really don't think so!

Evangelism is just another *sect* in the Christian faith that has drawn up its own definition for Christianity: you *have* to do it this way or you're not a 'true' Christian. In that, they are no different from all the other sects.

These kinds of irrational arguments are how many religious conflicts have started. This is why the troubles in Ireland with the IRA managed to last for so long – two religious sects, the Catholics and the Protestants, both of which are different forms of the same religion, Christianity, both of which use different forms of worship, disagreed. Violently disagreed.

For Muslims it's the same: the Shia Muslims absolutely *hate* the Sunni Muslims. But they are all Muslims.

Instead of distancing herself from other Christians, instead of saying that her 7%, the Evangelists, her so-called 'true' Christians, were being victimised in some way, this woman should have been acknowledging that she was part of the 84%, who basically believe what she believes – all that Jesus nonsense.

Instead, she decided to moan about being in a minority. In the USA, 84% of people, or thereabouts, call themselves Christian. Why not be grateful for that? In the UK, my home country, 72% of people say they are Christian but there are only about a hundred or so Evangelists in the whole country, and probably half of *them* are

Americans on holiday, so living in a country which is 7% 'true' Christian is something she really shouldn't take for granted.

If she moved over here, EC would probably be tempted to say that as little as 1% of the country was Christian, but where would be the reality in that argument? The UK, unlike the US, has an official state religion. No prizes for guessing that the official religion is one of the many branches of Christianity, the Church of England (which is itself part of a larger organisation, the Anglican Church). It's unlikely that the official state religion of any country would be Christian if only 1% of its population were Christians.

This attempt to alienate others who ostensibly belong to the *same* religion goes a long way towards demonstrating the intolerance for people of *other* religions that exists in the world today.

In case there is any doubt, I have no respect for the religious convictions of *any* religion, because they are based on out-dated myths and ancient scribblings. However, I am certainly not intolerant of the people themselves. I would not go to war to force atheism onto others, and neither would I remove anyone's right to pray to a non-existent fictional character. But by putting their own labels on people of their own religion, Christians have a history of division which is of their own making.

Only perfect people can join the club.

Another common tactic used to classify 'true' Christians is to deny that criminals are in fact Christians at all. There have been many studies about the religiosity of the general prison population, and for my examples I will look at US prison population surveys. In general every one of these studies show that the proportion of Christians in the population of the country as a whole closely corresponds to the number of declared Christians in the prison population.

This is what you would expect. In 1997, according to figures provided by the Federal Bureau of prisons, the prison population of the US was around 75% Christian. This matches the 75%[1] of the US population who call themselves Christian. The story is different for

---

[1] The 75% quoted here differs from the 84% referred to by EC, who was quoting from an unspecified survey she had seen.

atheists. The US is 10% atheist, but only makes up approximately 0.2% of the prison population. This would indicate that atheists are *less* likely to commit serious crimes, but this is not the point I am making here.

What some Christians, and again it is usually Evangelical Christians who make these statements, will say is this: 'Anyone who robs, steals, murders or commits any such serious crimes is not following the message of Christ, and is not really a Christian.'

Let me explain what this means. No bad person is a 'true' Christian. Therefore all Christians are good people. And since all Christians are good people, it means that the word of the Lord is helping them to live good lives. Hallelujah!

This really is straining the definition of what is a Christian and what is not a little too far isn't it? To these people Christianity is an elite club where only the righteous have any chance at all of fitting in. Forget all that 'forgiveness of sins' malarkey, if you're in jail, you're suddenly not in the Christian club anymore.

Well, let's take back the moral high ground shall we? I proclaim that the people in prison who say they are atheists are not 'true' atheists at all. This means that there are *no* atheists in prison. Ergo, atheists are all moral, upstanding citizens. Hurrah!

Bullshit.

And it's not just criminals who are not 'true' Christians. There is an even bigger group who have been told they can't call themselves Christians. How big? Is one sixth of the population, one billion people, big enough for you? First, some background about how I discovered this amazing distortion of the truth.

Christian persecution of the Jews.

Christianity has a long and bloody history of persecuting other religions, and perhaps the longest 'tradition' has been the persecution of Jews by Christians over the centuries. I made a YouTube video which dealt with the subject in some detail, covering a period from the 4th century AD, when Christianity came to power in the Roman Empire, right up to the year 1800, after which anti-Semitism started to become a racist issue rather than a religious one, and so was not as relevant to the point I was making.

Since the material used in the video was taken pretty much verbatim from the excellent web site at **www.religioustolerance.org**, there is no need to repeat the information here. I recommend you visit the site for yourself.[2]

Catholics are Christians? Surely not!

I expected there to be very few arguments about the facts themselves, because you can find hundreds of history books and look up the points I mentioned. The Christians *did* persecute the Jews, and those are the *facts*. You can cross-reference all the sources you want, but you won't find much to argue with.

So to be honest I was totally amazed when a heated argument began, again from comments posted by what I discovered were Evangelical Christians. I was told that:

Christians didn't persecute the Jews at all. Catholics did.

Take a moment for that to sink in. I hope that you're feeling as incredulous as I was when I first heard it.

Of course I quickly told these people that surely they must realise that Roman Catholics are part of the Christian religion? It would be like saying Baptists aren't Christian, or Methodists, or Evangelists, none of these are Christian. They're all just other branches of Christianity, and it's obvious that they are all Christians. Any other assertion is simply foolish and has no basis in reality.

Apparently not. Up to that point I must have led a very sheltered life, because I wasn't at the time aware that, apparently, Evangelical Christians are specifically taught that Catholics aren't Christians *at all*.

Obviously that confused me, because I always assumed that when I saw the Pope on TV he was in fact a Christian. He's usually wearing or holding a crucifix, and occasionally mentions God and Jesus, so those things are pretty good clues to his religion. When he prays, and he sometimes does it in public, I doubt if he is praying to Allah or Buddha. No, I'm pretty sure that the Pope believes in God and Jesus and that he's a Christian.

---

[2] www.religioustolerance.org/jud_pers.htm

But the people who said that Catholics aren't Christians were pretty adamant. Apparently the teachings of the Catholic Church aren't compatible with what's in the Bible, so that makes them non-Christian.

Evangelists don't like Roman Catholicism because they don't agree with the way that Catholics praise God, and they don't approve of some of the teachings of the Catholic Church. There are a lot of differences. A lot.

But then isn't that what religion is all about? You get together into an exclusive club that people can only join if they follow absolutely every rule in that club. That's why there are so many different denominations, or branches, of Christianity:

- Evangelists don't believe the same things that Baptists do
- Baptists don't believe the same things that Methodists do
- Methodists don't believe the same things that Quakers do
- Quakers don't believe the same things that Seventh-Day Adventists do

All these branches of Christianity, and there are hundreds of them, worship the same God, use the same book, the Bible, and have one-to-one chats with Jesus when they go to Church. And that includes Catholics.

None of them agree with each other 100%, which is why they give their branches of Christianity different names. That doesn't mean they aren't Christians, it means their form of worship of the Christian God is just different. The religion is the same, just parts of the doctrine change.

So the argument that Catholics aren't Christians is bullshit. I'd never even heard anyone say it before, maybe because I live in the UK, so like I said, it was a bit of a surprise to me.

But who do they imagine decided which books to put in the Bible? No surprises. It was the Catholic Church.

Who produced hand-written copies of the Bible over the centuries and made sure it survived until the printing press was invented and everyone could get a copy? Catholic monks in monasteries, that's who. And what was their religion? Christianity.

Who do you think thought up the actual word, Bible? The word 'Bible' isn't even in the Bible, it was the Catholic Church who decided to call it that. It's like the question 'what have the Romans ever done for us', but it's 'what has the Catholic Church ever done for Christianity?' And the list is enormous, covering century after century of history.

I'm not going to go any further into why Catholics should be called Christians, because I'm not here to defend any form of Christianity. I'm an atheist, so in my eyes they are all deluded, they all believe in a magic beardy man in the sky, and a big book of fairy stories, so I have no respect for any of them.

However, I do have total contempt for people who deny their own history.

When I made the video about the persecution of Jews by Christians, the intention was to show exactly how much it's possible for religion to encourage division and conflict. My views on atheism relate primarily to my knowledge of, and experiences with, Christianity, purely because that's the official religion where I live, and it's the biggest religion in the Western World. But Islam doesn't exactly have a great history of unity – the Sunni Muslims and the Shia Muslims are all Muslims but they kill each other ever day.

Whether or not you *now* believe that Catholics are Christians, the persecution of the Jews happened when the Roman Catholic form of Christianity was just about the *only* form of Christianity in Western Europe. So I'm saying with 100% certainty that Christians throughout the centuries have persecuted Jews, among others, and they did it in the name of Christianity.

The correct response from Christians would be this: we accept that Christians have done some terrible things in the past, but we hope that those things will never happen again. Christianity has moved on. It took 2000 years to work out that Jews shouldn't be persecuted by Christians, but Christianity got there in the end. That's what a sensible Christian response would have been.

But instead, the response was: 'the Catholics did it, and they aren't Christians. *We* aren't responsible, it was them'. And because Catholics aren't Christians, this means that Christians *never* persecuted the Jews. It never happened.

'It never happened.' Does that sound like a denial to you? Because it certainly does to me.

In Denial.

Denying that Christianity had anything to do with the massacre of Jews before 1800 sounds exactly like a person living in Germany denying that his country had anything to do with the massacre of the Jews in the 20th century.

If a German said that the Nazis might have lived in Germany but they weren't real Germans, would you believe him? What if someone told you that no German had *ever* killed a Jew in World War II, that it was the Nazis who did it, and they weren't true Germans?

So if you believe that the Nazis in the 20th century were real Germans, why do some people insist on saying that Catholics are not true Christians?

If your ancestors were slave owners, there can be no pride in that fact, but no denying it either. 'My ancestors did something which we now know to be wrong, and this is the lesson we have learned from history.' That should be your position if this is what your family history tells you.

To deny your history, particularly if it is a bloody one, is one of the worst crimes of negligence we can commit, because it means we can never learn from our mistakes.

The correct response to my earlier video, describing the persecution of Jews by Christians, would be to accept that these things happened, learn from the lessons of history, and move on.

The wrong answer is to put your head in the sand, blame things on some other group of people, even though you share the same history, and learn absolutely nothing. It's why Holocaust Denial is illegal in France and Germany, and many other countries. If you hide the truth, people keep on doing the same terrible things.

The information I gave in the video I made was a history lesson. It presented facts, verifiable information from history, and my intention was to show that religion, in this case Christianity, has a history of division and conflict and persecution.

But the people who said that Catholics are not Christians simply proved my point, and they made another point altogether. Not only is there conflict between different religions, there is also conflict between people of the *same* religion. People who worship the same God, follow the same holy book, and believe that Jesus came to save them, are *still* divided, distrusting of each other, and in denial over their own history.

Encounters with Christians like this just end up making my point for me, that religion is a bad thing, a negative thing, something that we should get rid of and live without.

To the Christians who actually agreed with me about Christian history and think that Christianity has learned its lesson about persecuting people, let's list a few things: murdering of abortion-clinic doctors by Christians, persecution of homosexuals by Christians… do I need to continue? Have lessons really been learned?

Of course, whether or not Catholics are actually Christians, the 'true' Christians all believe that since Jews never accepted Jesus as their personal saviour, all dead Jews, including those killed in the Nazi Holocaust, are currently being tortured in eternal Hell fire. Every persecuted Jew whose death the 'true' Christians claim was nothing to do with their religion, is being cruelly punished by the God of that same religion, purely because they were not 'saved'.

If there was one thing I learned, and which I'm now happy to share, it is that people who call themselves 'true' Christians, the ones who say that all the other Christians aren't actually Christian at all, those are the people who are the worst kind of ignorant religious fools.

7 More Deadly Sins

You can never have enough sins.

The original 7 deadly sins were:

- Pride
- Envy
- Gluttony
- Lust
- Anger
- Greed
- Sloth

But Christianity has moved on. For 'true' Christians the original 7 sins were just, well, too easy to avoid. 'True' Christians need new challenges, new temptations, new sins. 'True' Christians need to feel they really are 'Holier than thou'.

So to make them feel even more special, these are the 7 sins that all 'true' Christians *must not do*!

1. **Thinking**
   - Don't think.
   - Just accept.
   - Thinking is bad.
   - If God wanted you to think he'd have helped your brain's evolution along a little more. Know what I mean?

2. **Logic**
   - Logic hurts.
   - Avoid logic.
   - Logic is bad.
   - If God was logical he'd have pointy ears and his own death grip. There's no logic in the Bible, so why would God want you to use such a dangerous thing?

3. **Common Sense**
   - Not necessary.
   - 5 senses good.
   - 6 senses bad.
   - Common sense bad.
   - If Christianity made sense Jesus would have done a Houdini escape from the cross and found work in a back-street restaurant over the border.

4. **Rational Thought**
   - Rational smational.
   - Thought? See (1).
   - Rational thought hurts *and* it's bad. See a pattern emerging?
   - God tells us to avoid all sins that contain two or more difficult words. This one has three.

5. **Facts**
   - Facts imply science.
   - Science = logic.
   - Remember logic?
   - Avoid! Bad!
   - If God wanted us to believe facts he would have buried humans with the dinosaurs. There are no facts in the Bible!

6. **Proof**
    - God's appearing days are over.
    - Proof is tricky.
    - Avoid proof.
    - How much proof do you need that God's invisible unseen presence is everywhere?

7. **Tolerance**
    - Tolerate nothing.
    - Tolerate no-one.
    - Be a 'true' Christian.
    - If tolerance was in God's game plan he wouldn't have invented religion.

'True' Christians never allow thinking, logic, common sense, rational thought, facts, proof or tolerance. If they did, there would be no need for Christianity, and that would be a bad thing.
Wouldn't it?

11

God's Big Test

Punk'd by the Holy Spirit.

What if there is a God, and he's just playing with us? God is making it look like the Universe was created by the Big Bang, that evolution is how complex life formed on Earth, and he put all the fossils in order just to fool us. Why would he do that? Because it's all a big test of our common sense.

Everybody who actually *believes* in God, despite the vast mountains of evidence, evidence which shows that science is right about evolution and the origins of the Universe... all those people who choose God over science are just too *stupid* to get to Heaven because they are blinded by faith and have lost the ability to use their minds.

But those people who believe in science, the people who think God is a silly idea, those people get to go to Heaven. That's because only atheists have the intelligence that God is looking for. Atheists are the kind of people God wants to share Heaven with him. Because who would want to share all eternity with some crackpots who believe in all that miracle stuff in the Bible and yet don't believe the scientific facts staring them right in the face?

There's an obvious problem with this theory, because I don't believe it. And I don't want you to believe it either, because if you believe that God is testing you, you've already failed the test. If you believe in the invisible man in the sky, he'll think you're an idiot and he won't want you anywhere near him.

So my message to you is this:

Atheists go to Heaven. Christians, Muslims and Jews... go to Hell.

Are you serious?

Well obviously not. 'God's Big Test' is just a parody, which actually does a complete reversal of Pascal's Wager.

Pascal's Wager is a favourite of Christians, despite the fact that it is riddled with holes the size of, well, very big holes indeed. You are asked to make a wager, which has two choices:

You believe in God.
- If God exists, you go to Heaven. Your gain is infinite.
- If God does not exist, you have lost nothing. When you die, nothing happens to you. There is no after-life. Life simply ends.

You do not believe in God.
- If God does not exist, again you lose nothing. When you die, nothing happens to you. There is no after-life. Life simply ends.
- If God does exist, you will go to Hell because you did not have faith in God. Your loss is infinite.

The wager is meant to show that you may as well believe in God, because the worst possible case if you do is that life simply ends. Whereas the worst possible case if you do not believe is eternal damnation.

The crater-sized fallacies of Pascal's Wager are many. Here are just a few:

1. The wager assumes there are only two choices: the Christian God or atheism. But there may be other gods, and you may well choose the wrong one. Who is to say that the 'correct' religion isn't actually Islam? Or maybe it's a Greek God, Poseidon, and souls end up swimming endlessly in the sea.

    Either way, if you choose the wrong god and then come face to face with the right one, the one who's dealing out punishment, he is going to be *really* mad at you for picking the wrong religion. Of all the thousands of different gods that have ever been worshipped, how do you know you have the right one?

2. God may not hand out punishments in the expected way. This is the premise of 'God's Big Test'. In this case the 'safe' option would have been atheism – the worst case scenario was 'life simply ends'.

3. You can't fool God. Simply saying that you believe in him because it's the safest option will get you nowhere – remember, he can read your mind. If God exists and you're just pretending to believe in him, he'll know.

4. How can you choose to believe in God? I can no longer choose to become a Christian than I can choose to grow an extra arm. Only evidence for God's existence could change my mind, and there is little hope of that.

5. Maybe the worst case scenario for believing in God is that you waste your entire life worshipping, and so miss opportunities to do much more worthwhile, fulfilling activities. You may have a terrible life as a result of your choice, and if there is no God, you've sacrificed it all for nothing. In this case believing is not a 'safe' option.

But what if...

What if there is no Hell? What if everyone goes to Heaven, and God was just trying to make us behave ourselves by pretending he was building a big bonfire for us all?

He's benevolent, he'll forgive everyone. You'll all be in a place where you can't do any harm anyway, so why not just forgive and forget? After all, if you build an ant farm and the ants escape and start biting you, its not their fault, it's their nature.

Humans will naturally do 'bad' things from time to time. That's why we have laws make us think twice before we break them. That's why people are brought up by their parents to be good, to respect other people, not to steal, not to break windows, not to play in the street, not to talk to strangers.

So perhaps God accepts this. He made us just to watch us play and build and kill and live and die. Just like ants. God, the big invisible ant-keeper in the sky.

Who's to say it's not true? Can you prove it isn't true? No? Then by Christian standards of proof, it *must* be true, right?

But...

What if God doesn't even exist? No God, no Heaven, no Hell. Now there's an idea I can get to grips with. And it's no 'what if'. There is no God. He ain't there. Believe it. Or not – let's not argue over what an atheist is, okay?

Seek urgent medical attention.

Anyone who thought that this was a serious evaluation of a section of Christian doctrine would have to be really stupid to make those comments public wouldn't they?

Then why, when I put forward those ideas, did I get a flood of irate Christians criticising me for corrupting the message of the Bible? How dare I pervert scripture! Heaven does not work that way! And so on.

I can only conclude that the more religious you become, the less likely you are to have a sense of humour, or to be able to spot a joke. Even when I told them it *was* a joke, they were still unable to grasp the nature of the 'test'.

Is there such a medical condition as religion-induced dementia? If there is, it's becoming an epidemic and needs rapid action to prevent further spreading. I recommend a copy of this book be sold to every Christian on the planet. All for the good of mankind, of course. Any financial reward I receive is purely incidental!

12

Genocide is Never Out of Context

Ignore the nasty parts.

Christians are forever quoting passages from the Bible. I suppose it's part of the job description, so you can't really blame them. Whenever any question of morality comes up, or why God is the answer to all our problems, always rely on a Christian to come up with a brief verse, sometimes two or three, which they say proves the love of Jesus, or explains why God loves you.

But just you try to mention some of the passages where God kills thousands of people, or threatens to send people to Hell and torture them, or when Jesus says that entire cities will be burned if they don't like what he has to say.

What's the Christian reply to that?

'Out of context! Out of context!'

They tell you that you can't quote passages like that without reading the rest of the Bible. 'God is Love, and Jesus came to save us all, and the Bible is a testament to God's divine creation and his love for mankind'… you get the idea.

So Christians can quote out of context, but non-Christians aren't allowed to do that. Double-standards or hypocrisy, call it what you will, but while Christians don't seem to like sharing the bad parts of the Bible, they have quotes aplenty for the clean, sanitised areas.

Now try telling a Christian that God did a lot of nasty things in the Old Testament. That's probably the biggest Biblical understatement of all. The direct death toll at God's hands, and the Bible itself conveniently provides us with the numbers, is around 2.27 *million*. By comparison, Satan kills 10. Not 10 million, just ten people.

Bringing up these and other facts from the Old Testament will elicit a response along the lines of 'the New Testament changed all that, and

Genocide is Never Out of Context 75

now that Jesus has died for our sins the world has changed, so the Old Testament really doesn't apply.'

Hold on, the Psalms are in the Old Testament. The Lord is my Shepherd; I shall not want (Psalm 23) is always a Christian favourite. So that doesn't apply any more? And the Christians will say, 'Oh no, obviously *that* still applies. The Psalms are beautiful poems and verses about the Love of God.'

And the Ten Commandments. Can we ignore them because they are in the Old Testament? And the Christians will say, 'No, the Ten Commandments are God's holy laws and we base all of our own laws on them.'

So what about the bit in 2 Chronicles 14:12, when God personally kills a million Ethiopians?

Unsurprisingly the Christians will become almost apoplectic in their eagerness to cry foul on the very thought that God is a sadistic mass-murderer.

'Out of context! Out of context! You can't take quotes out of context, you have to read the whole Bible.'

And yet the Psalms and Proverbs can be quoted out of context, and the Ten Commandments, and passages from Deuteronomy and Leviticus, and the book of Daniel and Isaiah and Joshua. These are all regularly used in Christian sermons, without fear that they are 'out of context'.

So why can't we quote some of the death and destruction that God rains down on his enemies? Do they have something to hide? These passages are in the Bible. Why are they so touchy about repeating them?

What's actually happening is this. When Christians tell you to study the Bible as a whole, what they really mean is:

Ignore the nasty parts.

Try not to think of all the bad things God has done. Because overall, God is good. There's plenty of good stuff in the Bible. No need to bring up all that killing and smiting and burning of cities. And we don't want to mention the threats and the torture and the thoroughly nasty things that God did in the past, and threatens to continue doing in the future.

Let's just ignore the nasty parts and focus on that old favourite, 'God is Love'.

Well okay, in that case we should do that with everyone, shouldn't we? If this principle is good enough for God, can we apply it to people who have committed far fewer crimes? Let's take an example.

In Denial.

Here's a story about a man who was born in 1944. He was an English pop music singer who became famous in the 1970s. Between 1972 and 1995 he had 25 hit singles, with a total of 176 weeks in the UK Top 100. In 1984 he recorded one of the top 30 Christmas hits of all time. Before 1999 he was one of the most loved and respected stars in the United Kingdom, and had been so for over 25 years. He was a great character, loved by all generations.

No longer.

Because this is the story of Gary Glitter. His real name is Paul Gadd, and in 1999 at the age of 55 he was convicted on child pornography charges. In 2006 he was convicted again, this time for child sex abuse, and was locked away in prison, in Vietnam.

So for 55 years the story was a good one. It was only in the last 7 that it went down the toilet. Should we then take Gary Glitter's life as a whole and say that *overall* he's a great person? If I mention the child sex abuse charges is that 'out of context'?

Of course it's not out of context. Gary Glitter is a convicted paedophile, and you'll not find much sympathy for him anywhere. His music is still the same music, but in the last 6 years I can't remember a single time that it's ever been played on the radio. And you never hear his Christmas song, 'Another Rock and Roll Christmas'. It's the only UK Christmas song that nobody ever plays. Not ever.

How can you take evil, cruel or sadistic events out of context? You can't just forget what *people* have done, so why forget what *God* has supposedly done? A murderer is no less a murderer just because it was his first offence. And if you read the Bible, you'll find that the God described there has killed millions.

Killing every living thing on the planet except eight people and two of every animal makes the Holocaust seem like a birthday party by comparison, easily comparable with Saddam Hussein, Hitler, Stalin, or Pol Pot. And yet Christians still want to maintain that 'God is Love'.

Is this the same God who, when a group of children mock Elisha for being bald, sends out two bears, which proceed to rip apart 42 of those children (2 Kings 2:23-24)? As an aside, I found this analysis of the story on an Internet message board: 'God is perfect and holy while all people are imperfect sinners. Therefore, we will never know the ways of God unless He reveals them to us.' The morality of this (undoubtedly Christian) person just shines like a beacon doesn't it?

As soon as a Christian tells you that you've quoted a passage from the Bible out of context, you know that he simply has no other answer. Ask him to explain why God kills so many people in a certain passage. He'll say, 'Out of context, you have to read the Bible as a whole.'

Now ask him to explain a few lines out of one of Jesus' parables, and suddenly it won't be out of context, he'll go on for hours about the truth of God's love. Christians can talk and talk about God's good works, but they have no answer at all for the genocide, the destruction, the slavery, misogyny and racism in the Bible.

The Bible isn't true, it's just folklore and legend. But those legends tell the story of a nasty piece of work, a God who won't think twice about drowning all life on the planet. He's done that once already, and the Bible says he's planning to kill everyone again unless we all get down on our knees and praise him for being so utterly wonderful.

So send out a message to Christians: stop trying to convince people that God is loving and kind. The Bible says he's a mass-murdering butcher, and there's no denying it.

Of course, don't quote me on that – I might be taken out of context.

God Almighty's Genesis Diary – Day 2

Day 2 – Tuesday

8:30 am

Had a rotten sleep last night. Because I didn't have time to do anything with the water, the whole place is damp. What with the leaks, the drips, and my bed sheets soaked through (an unrelated incident which I don't need to discuss here), I was lucky to get more than a couple of hours shut-eye. I really need to separate the waters from the waters if I'm going to dry out this joint any time soon.

And the light I created, isn't it supposed to go off at night? This job is riddled with loop-holes. Just when you think you have it all working, you need to create things like a combo timer/dimmer switch, when you should be resting. I can see this isn't going to be as easy as I thought.

I'll be glad when the weekend comes, at least I get a day off.

9:45 am

Damp now fixed. Finally. It took a bit of figuring out but I eventually went for a cosy little firmament, which is big enough for now, but I'm thinking it will need some extending out the back. I'll see what jobs I have this afternoon and if I'm not too busy I'll make a start. I'm hoping there are going to be a few souls in there one day, so I'll need the extra room eventually.

Not sure what the building regulations are but as I am the One True God I expect it will be no more than a formality to get my plans passed.

What I've created so far is pretty cosy. I went for the minimalist look – the clouds theme was a given, but a few touches of gold and silver add to the ambience, I think. Heavenly.

9:50 am
I am so good. Heaven. I like it. I'll keep it.

11:15 am
Small problem with the water again. Since most of it's in empty space, it froze solid and the pipes burst, just outside the Pearly Gates I fitted earlier. Luckily I spotted the leak in time and a quick 'let there be sponges' got rid of most of the mess before it could stain the décor.

Decided to call in a plumber, just to be safe. Although I'm omnipotent, I really can't be bothered with this job, to be honest, and I'm sure a tradesman will do a much better job than I ever could.

He said he had a few other jobs on but I told him Thursday afternoon just wasn't good enough, so he's making an extra effort and told me he will call round later today.

3:30 pm
Still waiting for the plumber. Tried to amuse myself with a game of 'I Spy' with the Holy Spirit, but he's useless at this kind of thing and oh my God what a bad loser! Admittedly, this is only day two of Creation and there's not actually a lot to spy as yet, but he's not very bright if he thinks 'something beginning with W' will tax the Supreme Being for long.

It doesn't help that I'm all-seeing and all-knowing, but it's not *my* fault I have all the answers is it? He went off in a bad mood. Loser.

4:45 pm
No plumber. Tried to contact him but he's not answering his phone. Just you wait until I see him, I'll give him a piece of my mind. I've got his card, so tomorrow I will find a special place for this 'Mr Satan, Prince of Plumbers'. Somewhere warm, if you know what I mean.

6:15 pm
My second day on the job and I'm wading around in sludge up to my knees, fitting insulation to the Holy Water pipes so they don't burst again. And you know what I forgot? Central heating. So the only water available will just have to be cold. No way am I starting again on this one. It's dusk already, and I even had to invent that name for it because I wasn't anticipating working so long today.

7:30 pm

Finally finished the job, mopped the clouds, but I can't seem to get the grey stains out of some of them. At least Heaven will be dry for the foreseeable future.

With all this hassle it seems like I did very little today, so now I'm well behind schedule. And I missed my favourite soaps on TV, so now I'll have to watch the omnibus edition on Sunday. I *knew* I should have set the VCR.

14

How to Prove There Is No God

Admit Defeat!

If there's one subject that will get atheists into deep water more than any other, it's claiming that you can prove there is no God. So, before you waste any more time wondering how I am going to supply this proof, let me put the thought out of your mind.

I'm not. I can't. Nobody can prove that God does not exist.

That sounds a bit of a defeatist attitude coming from an atheist, but it's true. You can't actually prove that *anything* does not exist.

To prove that something does *not* exist, you would have to inspect every single particle in the Universe. God could be hiding under the stairs. He could even be in the closet. Or he could have come out of the closet and be hiding a billion light years away, somewhere we could never ever look.

We cannot prove that God does not exist.

So what does that mean? Nothing. It means nothing, it implies nothing. Atheism does not stand or fall on that statement.

This is because, by the same token, we cannot prove that fairies do not exist. We can't prove unicorns don't exist. We can't even prove that the dodo is extinct, because until we look under every bush, in every wood, every forest, every park, every piece of land in the whole world, we won't know for sure that the dodo really is extinct.

But surely we *know* that the dodo is extinct, don't we? We *must* know that a live dodo no longer exists.

Do we? We say we do, but the only reason we say the dodo is extinct is that there's no evidence that there are any more living dodos on the planet. Nobody has seen one, nobody has heard one. We haven't found any dodo feathers or dodo poo.

A lack of evidence leads us to assume that the dodo isn't there.

The Evidence for God.

So what about God? How much evidence is there that God exists? How many people have seen him recently? How many people have heard his voice, or recorded it so that we can prove that he's there? By scientific standards, is there any evidence that God exists?

We do have *some* evidence, but it's very weak evidence indeed. Prayer has a success rate of maybe 0.1%, which means that every time 1000 people pray, the chances are that one of those prayers will come to pass. But with a 99.9% *failure* rate, it's unlikely that we'll close down all the hospitals and build churches instead.

A 0.1% success rate could be achieved if everyone prayed to a lucky horseshoe, or an old carrot. *Coincidence* is what makes prayers appear to come true. If you pray that your sick mother recovers from surgery, remember to give at least *some* credit to the skill of the expert surgeon who did all the work. The presence of an invisible man hovering over the operating table probably has little to do with her fight for life.

Other weak evidence is in the miraculous appearance of God's face, or sometimes the image of the Virgin Mary, on burnt toast. Sometimes he might reveal himself on mouldy wood, or in the form of a divinely inspired root vegetable. Truly the power of God is beyond all belief! A bit of a comedown from the times when God made billions of galaxies without a second thought, isn't it?

There is, then, no *solid* evidence for God's existence. But does that mean he doesn't exist at all? No, because we haven't inspected every particle in the Universe. We cannot know that he doesn't exist until we do. And even then, the description of God includes a bit of a deal-breaker: he is beyond comprehension, a supernatural being impossible to detect, so on our God hunt we can't know if we just zoomed straight past him without even realising.

Yet by every standard of evidence that we have, we can logically conclude that God *probably* does not exist. This also means that Zeus might exist, but he *probably* does not. Thor might exist, but he *probably* does not.

Even Santa Claus himself *might* exist. Not at the North Pole, because we've checked, but he could be somewhere up in space where we haven't looked. It's possible. Remotely possible. But Santa Claus *probably* does not exist.

The fact that atheists cannot prove that God does not exist seems like a major victory for those who believe he's there. But it's not.

Just because you can't prove that something does not exist, this doesn't automatically mean that it *does* exist. You have to ask the question: is it *likely* that God exists? And given all the evidence – very, very little evidence for, and masses of evidence against – it really isn't likely that God exists at all.

Nobody witnesses miracles, praying does *not* cure the sick, it has *never* made amputated limbs grow back, and people who say that God has physically appeared before them and spoken to them are regarded as mad, even by religious people, who you'd think would give them a bit of credit for trying to provide some of the very proof that is lacking.

These religious people will rejoice in their 'victory'. They assume that having failed to prove our case for atheism, the alternative is that the Christian (or Muslim, or Jewish) God exists.

The burden of proof.

Who needs to supply proof in these cases anyway? Why should atheists need to prove that God does not exist? We don't make these claims. Religious people make these claims. The burden of proof is on them.

If I suggested to you that at the corner of every street are two invisible alien beings called Gunglies who report everything they see to the great Gunglefish in the sky, you would initially think I was mad, but then quickly ask for proof.

'No, you must prove that the Gunglefish is not there,' I would reply. 'If you cannot provide proof that he does not exist, your case is invalid. Let us pray to the Gunglefish, and may the love of his scaly body touch your heart.'

Of course this is madness. I have made an outlandish claim, which nobody should believe unless I provide positive and compelling proof. The burden of proof is on the person who makes such claims. It is not for atheists to prove that God does not exist, it is for Christians, or those of other faiths, to prove that he does.

There is another way to tackle the burden of proof argument, and that is to throw the very same 'logic' right back at the person demanding that you should be the one providing the proof. Next time you are asked to prove that the God of the Bible does not exist, use this simple argument:

I can't prove that there isn't a god.
Can you prove that there isn't *more than one* god?

To be able to show this, they have the same burden of proof that atheists have. They would have to inspect every single atom in the Universe, until they knew with absolute certainty that a *second* god, or even 10 or 20 gods, didn't exist. And again, supernatural gods may be beyond detection, so you could never really provide 100% proof.

Until it can be proven that there are no other gods, it cannot be proven that the God these monotheistic religions believe in is the only one out there. There could be a hundred, there could be a thousand. Look back to my discussion of Intelligent Design, where you'll see that there could be whole teams of gods, great factories in the sky, building all the animals and plants and people.

But is it likely? No.

Almost certainly, more than one God does not exist.

But for exactly the same reasons, it is *probably* true to say that no god exists, and with the evidence we have it is likely that there are no gods at all.

God the Suicidal Con Artist

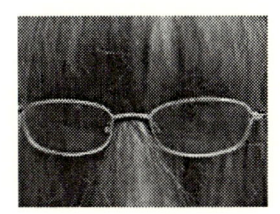

Build a man a fire and he's warm for the night. Set a man on fire and he's warm for the rest of his life.

A wise man

Wisdom from the wise. You know it makes sense.

Greetings. I am the wise man of the woods.

My hair gives me wisdom. My spectacles give me the gift of prophecy. And my chair gives me back ache. But I will be okay after a bit of yoga and some hallucinogenic drugs.

I bring you knowledge. But first I must ask you one question:

If God is all powerful and omnipotent, could he destroy himself and leave only a Universe which evolved following the principles of the Big Bang Theory and Evolution?

I will give you a moment to think about it…

Are you thinking?

Your moment is over.

I think the answer is… yes. This is what happened:

I think God got bored and committed suicide, but just before he pulled the trigger, he set a timing device so that the entire Universe would explode in a big bang.

No, bigger than that: a BIG Bang. Much better.

That is what the black holes are – pieces of God's shredded underpants spinning through the Universe. All the stars are sequins from God's ball gown, because he was a bit of a cross-dresser on the side, but in the end he could not find a dance partner so he blew himself up.

And therefore we conclude that the atheists are in fact correct: there is no God. However, there *was* a God, so the Jews got it right too.

But the Muslims and the Christians, you are completely wrong, and you're wasting your bloody time. As usual.

Ahah! But what if it's all a scam to claim all the insurance money? Hmmm… we think again… wise man of the woods in deep thought…

So, this insurance scam: God sneakily came back in disguise as his own son. 'That will work,' he thinks, and he comes down and he has a scout around, but the Romans spotted him, rumbled him, and guessed he was trying to cheat them out of the insurance money. And they did the right thing – they crucified the thieving little con artist.

Hurrah!

But it all backfired. God was *supposed* to be saved by the cavalry and cross the border to safety. But instead, he did not cross the border, the boards were made into a cross. And it was not the cavalry, it was the Calvary, where the cross was found.

Bummer!

Therefore, the sacred spectacles tell me that Jesus was in fact killed by… a typo.

Praise Jesus, for he is dead! And we will never have to suffer his voice again.

The wise man must now go, but he will return. See him at selected theatres from Friday. Because… you're worth it.

16

Animals Don't Need Bibles

Morals without religion.

As an atheist, resign yourself to constantly being told that atheists have no morals. How, in fact, can *anyone* lead a moral life which is not based on the teachings of the Bible? Religious life equals moral life. So says Christianity. While I will argue elsewhere that, actually, Biblical morals are far from the model behaviour we expect from our society, that is not the subject of this chapter.

First let me remind you that I'm an atheist, so it's fair to assume that I don't follow the teachings of the Bible, or its interpretations by present-day Christianity. That's not to say that none of the morals I have match with what Christians believe to be 'good', but that's the point – I think I lead a moral life, and yet I'm not a Christian. So where did these morals come from? Without God, how can atheists live a moral life?

Christians say that their morals come from the Bible. Other religions have their own sacred texts, so to a certain extent the same arguments apply elsewhere. Christians tell us that it's all laid out in the Bible and is plain to see. It's all God's work, part of God's plan for us. Live your life according to what is written in this book and you'll be rewarded, you'll go to Heaven. This, they say, is the moral code that you should use.

Another favourite Christian teaching: if we were all atheists we would have no morals. Ours would be a lawless society, full of shooting, killing, raping, stealing. If we didn't have that Bible, or the Qur'an, or whatever religious texts people choose to follow, if we didn't have God, we wouldn't have any morals.

How can we know that? Without erasing the knowledge of religion from our minds, how can we know that our behaviour would descend into anarchy if there was no belief in God? Are we, as atheists, following Biblical teachings without even knowing it (begging the question: so why read it at all?), and if so, how could we tell?

What we need to do is look at societies which are 100% atheist, and see how they function. This is of course impossible. Religion is part of every society on the planet. Every *human* society.

Animals are atheists.

If we cannot look at atheistic societies among humans, why not look at the societal behaviour of animals? What parallels can we draw from animal group behaviour? After all, humans are animals too.

Let's start with a very simple question: do animals have religion? More specifically, do they have a Bible? Do sheep have a Bible? What about foxes? Bears? Do any of these animals believe in God?

When you see lions basking in the sun, are they thinking, 'Oh, thank you God for giving us a tasty antelope for dinner'? Carnivores prey on other animals, but do they pray in church?

These questions may sound ridiculous, precisely because the answers are so glaringly obvious. There is no saviour for ants. Nobody will forgive the sins of the koalas. Dogs aren't going to Hell because they haven't accepted Snoopy into their lives. Animals don't have religion.

And yet they seem to get along just fine without it.

Do animals kill each other regardless of the consequences? Certainly they kill other species, but they do that for food, and of course humans kill animals too. But do animals regularly roam around killing their own kind? Such actions would obviously not be for food, but would be out of some kind of vindictiveness, implying a disregard for the welfare of their fellow animals.

Do rabbits kill other rabbits? Do we see whales killing other whales in underwater gang warfare? Serial-killing zebras?

Obviously this is not the case. In general, animals are pretty social creatures. Most species live in social groups, and even those animals which exhibit more solitary behaviour don't hunt down other animals of the same species out of spite, or for 'something to do'. They don't go around beating other animals over the head, or pushing them over the edge of a cliff.

Obviously there are exceptions, and you only have to look at your TV to see the wide variety of different animal societies and their behaviour patterns. If we're talking about social animals, what better example to take than any of the many species of monkey? Monkeys live in groups, and sometimes you see monkeys fighting each other. Sometimes you see them *killing* each other, monkeys killing other monkeys. This should not be strange to us because in the same way that we defend our territory, monkeys are territorial animals and sometimes the fight to defend this territory ends in injury or death.

If one pack of monkeys wanders into the territory of another, and they are not scared off by warning cries, monkeys will attack and, yes, may even kill the 'outsiders'.

But this is not evidence of immoral behaviour, merely disputes over territory. Killing is not high on the list of priorities. Live and let live is a better description of what is happening here – don't bother us and we won't bother you. Animals don't kill each other out of spite, out of vindictiveness, out of any sense that they just 'feel like' killing another of their species.

Territorial Disputes.

If territorial disputes sound familiar, this is because we humans exhibit the same reactions when others invade our territory. We fight back. If you jump into someone's garden or yard, chances are the owner will want you out of there. If you don't go, he'll start to shout at you, to begin with. If you still don't move, and depending on how aggressive he is, you might get a smack around the head, until you do move.

An example on a larger scale would be when one country invades another. In most cases the invaded people are going to fight back, and may not stop until the aggressor is removed, or some kind of agreement is reach. In animal behaviour we see many parallels with human behaviour. These are just the natural instincts of all animals. *We* are animals. Humans are animals.

I started by asking, do animals have religion? The answer is clearly no. Do they live in social groups? Yes. So if they can live successfully without religion, and we as humans wish to co-operate and live together successfully, why do we need a book to tell us what to do?

Why do we need a religious text that sets out our morals, when the morals that we need to live by are just the same morals that all animals are using to live in the animal kingdom?

Our morals are not determined by what we read in the Bible. They are a natural instinct, an animal instinct. A human instinct.

It's natural to want to live in a society where you feel relatively safe in the knowledge that nobody is going to attack you or kill you. To make sure this happens, we have all implicitly agreed not to do these things. I don't want somebody to kill me. I won't go out and kill anybody else. If everybody started killing everybody else, no one would feel safe. Society could not operate effectively, if at all.

If the society was totally anarchic, with no rules, we would not be able to live, because we would be immobilised with fear or, alternatively, consumed with aggression, just to stay alive.

The Golden Rule.

What is known as the 'golden rule', essentially 'treat others only as you wish to be treated' has its equivalent in all societies, even those which originally had no knowledge of Biblical teachings. It pre-dates and/or is independent of Christianity in many places.

Moral behaviour is *not* compliance with a set of religious rules, or with a collection of religious dogma. Moral behaviour is the reality of life in a social group, with accepted codes of conduct. It's just common sense to follow this way of life. Co-operation is the easiest way for a species to survive. This is not something that has to be written down and called 'religion' or 'the word of God'.

We have many written laws that penalise specific behaviour, but what underpins all of them is not religion. It is, rather, a social contract. That is true for humans, it's true for chimpanzees, for badgers, goats, lizards, fish, ants... the list is endless.

There are no Ten Commandments for lions. Thou shalt not covet thy neighbour's wildebeest? That's not written in a book. They don't *need* a book. No animals do.

Atheists don't need such a book. So why does *anybody* need a religious text to tell them how to behave, and what is 'moral' behaviour? Over time you might even say that these kinds of things have *evolved*, but then of course with evolution you enter into a whole different (though closely related) area of discussion.

Morals are in no way connected to religion. You can, of course, use religion in an *immoral* way. You can use it to justify all manner of atrocities, and there you'll find another long list. Of course atheists can behave in immoral ways too, but you cannot say that *all* (or even most) atheists behave immorally. You can be a bad atheist, you can be a good atheist. You can be a bad *Christian*. And of course you can be a good Christian, nobody would dispute that.

But the bottom line is that you don't need to have that Bible to be a moral person. You don't need to believe in God to be a moral person. This is how atheists live, and for the most part we have no problems at all with our morals.

17

Preaching Hatred

Gay pride.

I am gay.
 I say that without shame, I say that without fear. However, I say it without truth. Because I'm not gay at all.

But if I was, what would you say? What would you do? How would you feel? To Christians: how would the congregation of your church look upon me?

There are two subjects other than religion that will stir my emotions as surely as if you'd pushed the end of a lit cigarette into my face: racism and homophobia. Though there are racists in Christian churches, that is not what Christianity teaches. So I'm not going to talk about racism.

But Christianity, that religion of love and peace, of tolerance and joy, of so many supposedly positive aspects, but all of which fully deserve a healthy dose of 'inverted commas' around their names, is, at its core, and as part of its central message, undeniably and unashamedly intolerant, insensitive and hostile to anyone who is gay.

I want to tell you a story, the only story I know about this subject that is anywhere close to a first-hand experience. I'm not going to pretend to have dozens of gay friends, because I don't. I don't know why that is, but then I don't have many friends with ginger hair, or any Swedish friends at all. That's just the way it has turned out in my life.

But you don't need to experience bigotry and intolerance first-hand to know what it is and why it is wrong.

This is a true story and it happened to someone on YouTube, whose videos I had been watching for a short while. I enjoyed watching her because she was always happy, sometimes in a crazy way, but that's the kind of people I like – people who aren't afraid to play the fool while they're having fun.

Her name is Gina and she wants me to use her real name, and I'm happy to do so.

From Gina's videos it is obvious that she is a loving mother, and she is proud of her kids, who were occasionally seen on her videos. From what I could tell, and this was easy to see, they have every ounce of her love of life in them, and the whole family just looks like a happy bunch of people.

During the holiday season, around Halloween, she started a project, her holiday project, which was to make stuffed toys – teddy bears – to comfort sick children, to make a difference to their lives. They were for an organisation near to her home, which provides places where families can stay with their kids, close to the hospital, when they need treatment. People who saw her appeal for help sent in money for bears, and we all watched them being made and delivered, in her videos.

When she went to deliver the second batch of bears, the woman in charge told her to take the bears away and that she didn't want anything to do with Gina. She refused to work with her, ever.

Why? What could possibly motivate someone to turn away the offer of help – cute, cuddly bears which would benefit small children with serious illnesses, kids who were sick, far from their own homes, and in need of some comfort and just a little kindness and love? Why would she do this?

Quite simply, she discovered that Gina is gay. The woman, this 'representative' of a national charity organisation, would rather take toys away from sick children if it meant that she could avoid working with someone who is gay.

I find this kind of attitude to gay people sick and disgusting in so many ways. And there is nothing I can say which adequately expresses my contempt for someone who could take charity from a child because of her own personal prejudices against another individual's sexual orientation.

I cannot claim to know that the woman who worked at the centre for sick children and their families was anti-gay *because* she was Christian. I don't know. However, what I have told you so far has illustrated the damaging effects that homophobia can have on individual lives. This was an anti-gay action. The Christian Church is anti-gay. Someone, somewhere, someone with a heart as big as Gina, is today being shown just as much hatred by Christians, let there be no doubt.

God hates fags.

It angers me to see those three words: God hates fags. It's the name of a so-called 'Christian' organisation that is admittedly at the extreme end of the anti-gay religious spectrum. But that doesn't excuse anyone else, from moderate Christians through to Fundamentalists, who say that homosexuality is an abomination, that God hates homosexuality and, let's tell it exactly the way many Christians understand it, God hates fags.

From Genesis to Revelation there are over twenty different references to homosexuality in the Bible, all of which preach absolute intolerance and condemnation. Homosexuality is an abomination, according to Leviticus 18:22. If a man lies with a man, he should be put to death, says Leviticus 20:13. Old Testament not relevant? Let's try the words of Paul, one of the founders of Christianity, who in 1 Corinthians 6:9-10 lists ten things which will keep you out of Heaven. Of course homosexuality is one of them.

These passages are used by Christians to harass, oppress, intimidate and victimise homosexual people. Homosexuality, Christians clearly preach, is a sin. It is unnatural. It is something that gay people should recognise as a sin and ask Jesus for his forgiveness.

How can I explain how wrong this is? Consider these statements:

- I will not work with you because you are black.
- I will not work with you because you are female.
- I will not work with you because you are Jewish.
- I will not work with you because you are disabled.
- I will not work with you because you are gay.

Which of these do you find acceptable? Which of these views will bring down the anger of society, maybe even get you arrested, if you say it in public? Take care that nobody hears you if you say any of the first four. Simply go to church if you want to hear the fifth.

How many other ways are there to describe the evidence that Christianity is a religion of persecution and hatred? Christians may have persecuted the Jews for over 1500 years before finally realising that maybe, just maybe, 1945 was a good year to stop, but this is the 21st century now, and the Christian-led gay-bashing rhetoric continues, seemingly undiminished.

I tell this to everyone who wants to listen:

If a child of mine came home one day with a friend and told me he wanted to 'come out', the first thing I would ask him would be, 'You're not a Christian are you?' I just hope that if such a thing happened he would say these words to make me sigh with relief:

'No Dad, don't worry, I'm not Christian. I'm gay.'

Gina donated all her bears to a different charity, so that the same number of children could benefit from her, and her children's, hard work, and from the money that was donated by good people around the world. She is still posting videos and still smiling.

Footnote.

Christians say that homosexuality is a choice, that you are not born gay, and it is wrong to say that gay people have no choice about their sexual orientation. They preach eternal damnation for consenting sexual activity between a loving couple, just because they are of the same sex.

Those who support gay rights will usually maintain that no, it is something that is built into you at birth, so you can do nothing to change it. There is certainly compelling scientific evidence to suggest that this may be the case.

But is this the right argument to be making? Aren't we missing the point? Because even if it is a *choice*, what right has anyone to say it's wrong? If you're straight and Christian, why do *you* care what goes on between two consenting adults in their own home? If they're going to be damned (they're not), so what? It's not your problem.

I'd like to see more people defending not the science – is it natural or is it a choice? – but the right of individuals to *want* to be gay. The expression 'gay pride' wasn't chosen for nothing. Christians, cast your first stone elsewhere.

This is one of the core beliefs of Christians, that they have the right to tell you and I, and everyone else, what is moral, what is wrong, what is sinful. It's written in the Bible. It's the word of God. Well, Christians should read *these* words, written in *this* book:

Mind your own business.

18

The True Meaning of Christmas

Huddle around the Hell fire and listen, children…

Hello children. Christmas is a time for stories, and some of the best fairy tales ever written are found in a big old book called the Holy Bible.

Today I'm going to tell you a story about the very first Christmas, which happened even before religious people started to complain about signs saying 'Happy Holidays'.

Long ago and far away, in a town called Nazareth, there lived a young woman called Mary, who was engaged to be married to Joseph, a local carpenter.

Now although Mary was still a virgin, Joseph had been to second base a few times already, and technically a blow job didn't count under ancient Jewish temple law.

One day someone who called himself the 'Angel Gabriel' arrived in town. Gabriel had heard about Mary's love of 'kosher meat', and went to see Mary. He waited until he knew that Joseph was away on business for a couple of days and wouldn't disturb them, but told Mary that 'God had sent him' and that he had a message for her.

Mary was sceptical. 'Look, I don't want a copy of the Watchtower, so just fuck off and talk about God somewhere else.'

But Gabriel persisted. 'Mary you have been chosen to have a special baby. The baby will be the Son of God and you will call him Jesus.'

Mary started to get worried. 'Seriously, I don't know what you've heard about me but I don't turn tricks any more. I'll give you a quick hand job for twenty shekels, but that's all you're getting'.

Gabriel knew that time was short, so he knocked Mary lightly over the head with one of Joseph's hammers, and dragged her inside where nobody could see.

The True Meaning of Christmas   97

Next morning Mary woke up with a banging headache. Her clothes were all messed up, and beside her was a turkey baster, which she didn't recognise. Her lady lips felt a little bit sore, so straight away she put two and two together.

'The bastard!' said Mary. For God's love was now inside her.

Several months later, after a rushed wedding and a host of dubious excuses to Joseph and the neighbours, the happy couple set off to Bethlehem for the honeymoon. Joseph was still a bit confused about how Mary had managed to be with child, but she assured him that you could *definitely* become pregnant by swallowing it.

The honeymoon was all booked, but at the last minute the travel company went bankrupt, so the horse and cart was cancelled and Mary had to ride on a donkey. Worse was to come, because Joseph had forgotten to confirm the hotel booking, and when they asked about their rooms, the innkeeper told them to sleep in the pig sty.

Mary whispered in his ear, took him to one side for ten minutes, then returned, wiping her hand and telling Joseph that they had been upgraded to the stables. Mary knew that if she hadn't been pregnant she could have got them the penthouse suite, but the innkeeper didn't do fat girls, so the stables it had to be.

Joseph and Mary were both exhausted and fell asleep. That night Joseph had a strange sex dream involving a short woman wearing a white coat, but when he woke up all he could see was a sheep with a worried look on its face, and some wool inside his underpants.

Mary was in pain and told Joseph she was about to pop the baby out. Joseph held her hand and told her to breathe deeply and it would be alright.

'You fucking breathe you stupid fucking bastard, it's got a fucking head like a fucking beach ball. Get this fucking baby out of me!' said the blessed 'virgin' Mary.

And it was so.

The baby was born on Christmas Day, which meant that he should now get two sets of presents on one day, but most people would just save money and buy him one big one.

'Jesus Christ that fucking hurt,' said Mary. And hearing this, Joseph said that sounded like a good name for a baby, so that was that sorted out.

Over on a hillside some shepherds had been drinking and decided to go into town for some hot sex action. They found no women at such a late hour, but from the stable where Mary had given birth, they heard the bleating of a sheep. 'Hear that lads? Lamb sandwich tonight!

Mine's the one with the prettiest face!' and they burst into the stable, with their big shepherd's crooks held tightly in their hands.

'What the fuck are you doing here?' said Joseph. Can't you see my wife's given birth to the Son of God?

The shepherds looked at each other knowingly and nodded, for they had heard this prophecy before. 'Gabriel!' they agreed, 'The crafty bastard!'

Meanwhile three Wise Men had been following a bright star in the sky.

'I'm telling you, it's a fucking meteorite,' said one of them.

'And I say it's Venus in conjunction with Mars,' said another.

'You'll get Venus shoved right down your throat,' said the third. 'Stop arguing, I think we're here.'

The first wise man read the sign: 'Son of God Hotel. This is the place. But where's the baby?'

Wise man number two pointed to another sign. 'Deliveries round the back. Come on, they're in the stables.'

'Mind that cow shit!' ... 'Too late.'

What happened then was not nearly as funny as that scene from Monty Python's Life of Brian, so we take up the story much later.

King Herod heard about the birth of the King of the Jews, and he sent his men to kill all the babies in Bethlehem. Although they tried to escape, Jesus was sadly killed, so Joseph and Mary had to adopt.

He was a lovely little boy from an orphanage in Malawi, who they also called Jesus, and he grew up to be responsible for all kinds of wars and arguments, before being put to death after a dispute over Easter eggs.

And that is the story of the Nativity.

So remember, when someone brings a Christmas message to your door, stab them through the chest with a kitchen knife – they're only there because they've come to rape you.

Merry Christmas everybody!

19

A Sinner from Birth to Grave

Sin is a Christian concept.

Here's a message I received from a Christian. This person was an atheist who became a Christian, but I'll take this opportunity to note that we are all born as atheists. Some of us simply manage to stay that way.

Atheist-to-Christian converts are the worst kind because they are the ones who have personally witnessed the power of Christ flowing into their bodies (which hole he uses to enter you is not clear, but I'm thinking 'back door') and they want to tell you all about it. Much like the annoying zealots who give up smoking and then deliver serious ear-bashings to those who dare to walk within ten feet of them while carrying a lit cigarette.

After the customary minor insults, he told me in no uncertain terms that I was the kind of person who was sinful and, furthermore, that I didn't want to give up my sin and be accountable to anyone or anything.

As I write, I live alone, work from home on my own projects to make money, and since there is no God, why would I need someone to be accountable to? Accountable? What does that even mean? You mean that every bad thing I ever do has to be written down in a big book and added up when I die? Er, apparently that's exactly what some Christians believe: God's big book of naughtiness. I forget the real name, but my description would seem to fit just as well as any other.

But for me the clincher was his 'accusation' that as long as I believed there was no God, I could continue to do whatever I wanted as long as it did not hurt anyone.

Well excuse me for pointing this out, but is there anything actually *wrong* with leading your life based on that kind of philosophy? Isn't this, again, the 'golden rule', ie 'treat others only as you wish to be treated'? This can also be interpreted as 'don't do anything to hurt anyone'.

Remember, he was accusing me of being so morally bankrupt that, as an atheist, I could do anything I wanted just so long as nobody was harmed in any way, physically, emotionally, financially or otherwise.

Meanwhile, if you *do* believe in God, Christianity teaches that *even if* you don't hurt anyone else, you are *still* wrong. This delightful concept is known as sin, an invention cooked up by religion to make otherwise good people feel *guilty*.

This misguided Christian believes that atheists do things that don't hurt anyone, and yet is implying that this is wrong. How can it possibly be wrong if there is no harm?

Let's say I'm alone in my home and I accidentally trip over the furniture and hurt myself. The odds are pretty good that a string of expletives will follow, directly proportional to the amount pain I'm suffering: 'Ow! Fuck! That fucking hurt! What bastard put that chair there? Ooo, Jesus Christ, my fucking arm hurts! Shit!'

Nobody is around. Nobody saw me. Nobody heard me. So why is my bad language something I should be ashamed of? In about two minutes I'll have forgotten all about it.

But if I was a Christian I would have to spend half an hour apologising to God for swearing, losing my temper and taking 'the Lord's name in vain':

'Sorry Jesus, I called you some naughty names but I didn't mean it, please forgive me. I pray for the sake of my immortal soul. And while I'm here, please bless my cat. Amen.'

Bullshit! This is not 'sin', it's *guilt*, and Christians are full of it. Among other things.

Let's try a mini-quiz:

- Who are the only people telling us that we are sinners?
  Answer: Christians

- What does the Christian church say can help out the sinners?
  Answer: Christianity

So Christianity invents the disease, then provides you with the cure. But without Christianity, you wouldn't have had the problem to begin with. Sins, to Christians, are what life is all about, and we're not just talking about major law-breaking here. Everything is a sin. Christianity says that we are all born into sin.

Imagine that. A religion which teaches that from the very moment we enter the world, we are broken, we are damaged goods, and we need faith in a fictional spirit to fix us.

The concept of sin is a crippling, debilitating mind-fuck, a disease invented by Christianity, a bullshit notion which Christians spend their whole lives feeling guilty about.

Any adult who tells you they have never felt lustful thoughts is a liar, and yet that's a sin. But who can possibly be hurt by someone's *thoughts*? Masturbation? Hey, you're going to need *major* forgiveness for that one, you little sinner you. Beg forgiveness from each and every one of those little swimmers you just launched into the cruel world.

What happens when others are involved? Just because you don't pray to the invisible man in the sky for forgiveness doesn't mean you can't recognise when you really *have* had a negative effect on someone else. And then you are accountable to *that* person, and only that person. You apologise. You try to put things right. If you can't put it right, then you can justifiably feel guilt, remorse, regret, because you made someone's life a little worse. And you have to live with those mistakes and hopefully learn from them. God is nowhere in the picture.

But if you have no effect whatsoever on anyone else, why should you ever feel that this is a sin? Thoughts are *never* sinful or wrong because they hurt no one (although the people who think that God monitors your every thought ought to be *seriously* paranoid). Actions can be wrong, but there is no higher power looking down on you. If you mess up, the onus is on you to put things right.

Let's re-visit what that Christian told me:

> As long as you believe there is no God, you can continue to do whatever you want as long as it does not hurt anyone.

I think I can live with that. How about you?

God Almighty's Genesis Diary – Day 3

Day 3 – Wednesday

8:50 am

Up and at 'em! I can feel that this is going to be a big day and I'm ready for anything. I'm going to check the schedule, get organised, maybe even get ahead of myself. If I'm lucky I might even get this whole thing done a day early, and that's two days' fishing time instead of one! I am truly all-powerful – see how easy this is?

9:15 am

You cannot be serious. Okay, when I left the office yesterday I had a quick look at the Wednesday file and all I saw was something about gathering the water in one place and making some dry ground. That was it. I knew what I was planning to do today, and it was all good.

But WTF is this?

Memo	Installation of all vegetation, including plants and trees must be completed before 5:00 pm Wednesday, ready for inspection shortly thereafter.
	By order of The Higher Power™
Note	Baal was the winner of the office sweep-stake. Next week's prize will be a set of steak knives.

Tell me this is wrong. Tell me I do not have only one day to make every species of tree. One day? Do they think I have some sort of magical powers? I can't just make this stuff out of thin air. Jeez.

I'm calling the office. This isn't fair. I get no advance notice of things like this. If I'd know about it I could have brought in some outside help, but there you go again, how am I supposed to find out without knowing the future? I really do get treated like shit in this job.

9:40 am

I booked a call with His Wonderfulness for 11:00 am, but I know what he'll say: we all have to pull together, these things are for the greater good. Yada yada yada. So on that assumption I am going to have to make a start anyway.

10:00 am

At least the water is all in one place now, and the dry ground is where it should be, so there's somewhere to put those bloody plants. I really think I made too much water though – half the planet is covered in it, and it keeps falling off the edges. Maybe I can round off the corners of the cube and see if that solves things.

10:25 am

A bit of a botch job that. I cut some bits off, but I had to smoosh things down, and now my nice smooth landscape is all bumpy. And it's dried rock hard, so I can't really do much with it now. I tried sanding it, and filing it down, but in the end decided to go for the 'rustic' look. Sort of olde worlde, 4 billion years old in fact. You'd really think it was that old, going by appearances.

Well it was either that, or spend time I haven't got fixing the damn thing, making it look pretty. Who's to know? And you can be sure nobody's going to doubt my capabilities as a designer.

10:50 am

Made five species of bush and a few root vegetables, which has taken me a good half hour. Oh dear. Oh shit. This is not going to happen by 5:00 pm.

The big man faxed me again just now – 'get on with it or else' seemed to be the gist of it, but there were some very colourful Hebrew words in there that I'm sure you can't say in polite company. His secretary cancelled the call I booked, and seemed oh-so-Holy when she spoke to me. I must remember to invent some diseases in her name. Bitch.

11:45 am

Drastic times, drastic measures. Pull out the Yellow Pages and look for 'Tree Gods'. Osiris. No, he left and became god of the dead. And he would have been my top choice too. Shame. Dionysus, he's in rehab after drinking all the wine offerings, so no to him too. Hold on, who's this? Demeter? 'Queen of the fruitful earth. Specialises in corn, but all jobs considered. Reasonable rates.' It's worth a shot. I don't usually work with women, I don't think it's their place to be in this business, but I am desperate.

12:00 pm

Did I say woman? I pulled up her web site and she's built like a brick shit-house. Dainty little fingers though. One quick call and she was round on her cloud in minutes. Impressive. I now have 100,000 species of trees on order, 250,000 plants, and some nasty looking stuff that she said was called 'fungus'. Apparently it's the next big thing, and she took one look at the dog's dinner I'd made of the planet and said her mushrooms would paper over the cracks a little bit. I even got some moss thrown in, no extra charge.

Here's the catch. Her union wants equal worship time for a minimum 4,000 years, and that includes all associated deities and spirits. Non-negotiable. The balls of Almighty God were well and truly gripped by the nut-cracker today, I tell you.

I signed. It's done.

3:15 pm

Tough time waiting, knowing that 5:00 pm is the ultimate deadline. I thought we had another Satan no-show situation here, but the girl has done me proud. I have boxes and boxes of greenery everywhere, plus one huge tub of growth activation powder, 'to be sprinkled liberally over Creation'.

I'm off. Planting I can do with my eyes closed. Turn up the volume on my gPod and we are on cloud nine, destination Earth.

3:25 pm

Too much fog, not enough cloud, they're all grounded. I took the number 34 lightning bolt instead.

4:50 pm

This is not to be repeated to anyone. Santa's sleigh was parked there, right outside the east entrance to Heaven, and I needed something to get the those trees spread around the place in double-quick time didn't I? You tell me, what else could I do?

He is going to go ape-shit when he finds out I took it. Sap everywhere. Everywhere. I'm trying to scrub it off the seats but with no cleaning products I'm stuffed. My hands are sore, my back is hurting and look at the time!

5:15 pm

The evil sadistic bastard. This from a hand delivered message, given to me just now:

> **Memo** Am giving you the benefit of the doubt, but trust that your greenery is in place. No inspection today, but you can contact me at my club until 10:00 pm if you have any questions.
>
> Yours, The Higher Power™

If he wasn't immortal I'd...

7:30 pm

Aphrodite is coming over. I need to work out some of this aggression, and if you knew her you'd know she gives the best work-out money can buy. That's right, I pay for it, but only because the ladies are intimidated by me. I could get any woman, but this way it's no strings attached.

Chains and ropes yes, but that's between me and her.

21

Who Do You Think You Are?

Something from my past.

I have a very crowded house. I hoard things. Junk fills my walls and floors. But perhaps the most surprising possessions I have are a number of music memorabilia items from the late 1990s. Unusual, perhaps, because they are items relating to that well know British pop group, the Spice Girls.

I have Spice Girls stuff all over the place – books, CDs, pictures on the walls of my office, videos, even a few of the Spice Girls dolls they used to sell. The full works. So you're probably expecting me to have some sort of dark secret, like I was a big fan or something, but it's not what you expect. For one thing, I don't look like a typical Spice Girls fan, and my taste in music is firmly towards the 'metallic'!

You'll find out why this relates to atheism shortly, so don't skip ahead. It's a personal story that I find helps to explain many things.

In the mid 1990s I was in a pretty bad way. I had self-esteem problems, I'd been pointed at all my life for being tall, and for wearing glasses – the usual things for a kid at school, but for some reason when I got older I wasn't able to cope with it all. I walked out of my job, I couldn't function at all. I was just sad and depressed all the time.

Unfortunately when you're vulnerable, that's the time when people can take advantage of you. Even so, if someone had come up to me and said the usual stuff about letting Jesus into your life, I would have told them where to stick it. I'm an atheist. You'd expect nothing else.

So, what else are single men with self-esteem problems vulnerable to? Obviously: women coming on to you. I won't go into too many details, but basically I kind of fell into a relationship with someone, and it was great for a couple of weeks. One thing about her that seemed a bit odd was that she would never want to see me in the daytime, not even at weekends, but I didn't think anything else of it.

Eventually she told me that she was part of a kind of charity group that helped people through some tough times in their lives, and she thought I might like to be part of it. I wasn't all that keen, but I said I would go along just to meet her friends there.

The meeting was at an old house somewhere at the edge of the town centre. It looked quite run-down, but inside it was clean enough, and in the living room were a couple of rows of chairs, and about half a dozen people just talking amongst themselves. My girlfriend told me to sit down and wait for a while, and everyone else took a seat nearby.

All of a sudden she came back in wearing a long yellow thing, it sort of looked like a toga or a sari, something like that. It turned out that she was not just a member, but actually the person in charge of the group. She stood in front of everyone and gave a talk about how friendship was important, but there were things in the world that were bad for society, stuff that was harmful to children, and that we needed to put a stop to it.

I'm probably not able to adequately convey to you the sense of how compelling it was to me, but I was in a relationship with her, it was pretty new so as you can imagine I was a little starry-eyed. Like I said I had been at a low point in my life, so I was probably more susceptible to accepting whatever I was told. Why would I not believe what she was telling me?

In case you're wondering where the Spice Girls stuff comes in, she told me after the meeting that the group wanted to make a change to young people's lives, and stop all the nonsense that music and fashion was teaching to young impressionable kids. It was robbing them of their innocence, she said. So all the volunteers would cut up pictures of famous pop stars, write the word 'EVIL' on them, and post them on lamp-posts or doors, near to shops and schools where kids would hang around.

Obviously, in the mid-to-late 1990s the Spice Girls were the big news item at the time, so my girlfriend said they were concentrating on the Spice Girls image, and how bad it was, how little kids were dressing up and going mad for the Spice Girls.

She showed me a room that was piled high with Spice Girls books and magazines, and other memorabilia – if you were there you'll know that the Spice Girls authorised the sale of all kinds of crappy merchandise at the time. She wanted me to help her cut up the magazine and make some of the notices they were posting up.

It all seemed a bit weird to me, and to be honest with you, the only reason I went along with it was that she was my girlfriend. Hormones again! For about two weeks that's what I did. We went round the local area, sticking little signs up everywhere, and we even made it into the local newspaper because everyone was talking about them – nobody knew where they had come from.

There were about ten of us in the group, and every couple of days she would give another little talk, and we'd make more posters and signs, and secretly stick them up when it was dark. It all sounds very small scale, and there certainly wasn't any big organisation behind this.

What happened next was that one of the people in the group was caught posting the signs. Unfortunately he told the police about the house where we all met, and my girlfriend was arrested and charged with criminal damage. I was questioned as well, but they didn't charge me with anything.

Unfortunately she really couldn't cope with the situation. She genuinely thought they were stopping her helping the children, and she took an overdose of sleeping tablets and she died. I guess she had other problems, but so had I, so I didn't recognise what was going on in her life and how much the project meant to her.

That opened my eyes to how ridiculous this all was. Someone died because they thought the Spice Girls were evil? What the fuck was that all about?

I kept some of the Spice Girls memorabilia and I keep it in my room to remind me of her. Obviously I don't believe in an afterlife so she's gone for good, but I don't think there's any harm in keeping someone's memory alive.

She was misguided, and she led me down the same path, and that's not going to happen to me again. It wasn't really a religion, and you couldn't even call it a cult, or maybe you could. There were only about ten of us, and I see one or two of them around, but they don't talk to me. Sometimes they just nod and keep walking.

I like to think I'm not nearly so vulnerable as then, but you never know. I lead quite a solitary life now, and am very careful about the relationships I have with other people.

I doubt if you were expecting a story quite like that one, but there you have it, another aspect of my life.

The lesson from this story may not be immediately obvious, until I tell you one more thing. This was *not* a true story.

When people manipulate your emotions they can sell you any kind of lie. If you felt upset for even a second that my 'girlfriend' had killed herself, it was because I sold you the lie.

People will tell you some amazing stories, and they will try to manipulate your emotions. Religions and cults are among the many organisations and people able to use your emotions to sell you their 'truth'.

Scepticism is healthy, and better people than you or I have been suckered into believing that something is real when, upon later reflection, the signs were all there to say that it was not.

Stay sharp.
Question everything.
Think.
And always remember: the Spice Girls are *evil*. That part is true.

I posted this story as a video on YouTube after I'd already become quite well known for my views on atheism. It was a risk, and I knew that I was up for some major criticism, which was exactly what happened. Of course in demonstrating that people play with your emotions, I was doing exactly that, and if you reacted strongly upon reading it you may feel that way too.

I was told by one person that I was not worthy to see the 'higher levels' of atheism, which sounded a little like membership of the Freemasons, so I will gladly rest on my ignorance if that is the case!

But there are easy lessons and there are hard lessons, and there is no one way to teach or to learn. If you don't take risks, if you don't see how far you can take an idea, you may achieve nothing at all.

Unlike a cult, or a religion such as Christianity, my words will have no lasting damage. You did not find out years later that it was all a lie. You turned the page and there it was.

22

Single Cell to Christian in 6000 Years

The oxymoron that is Christian science.

Some words of advice: do *not* try to give scientific evidence to someone who believes the Earth is only 6000 years old.

Don't even bother. Don't go there. Don't try it. Don't do it.

It won't work.

These people are experts at ignorance. They are like factual magicians – they can turn any known fact you give them and turn it into an argument for the Genesis story.

Even Jesus on a good day would struggle to take an entire world *full* of historical and scientific evidence and find proof that it's all wrong, that every single scientist on the planet was having a bad day when he submitted his life's work to peer review and rigorous scrutiny by the scientific community.

No, it takes a special brand of idiot to believe that the Earth is 6000 years old, and these are the Young Earth Creationists. A long title, and it's tempting to use the abbreviation 'morons' but for this chapter I'll simply shorten the name to 'Creationists'.

Creationists believe that every single piece of evidence, if it contradicts the Bible, is wrong. Every one. It's not just evolution, it's physics, chemistry, biology, astronomy, geology, archaeology, history… you name the field, they'll find an entirely opposite explanation and use it to discredit the facts. There are no concessions to science, not so much as a 'maybe the evidence has a point there'. Nothing.

If you find a piece of evidence that doubts the age of the Universe, they will pull out the classic statement, 'That evidence is wrong because scientists say…'

For example, 'scientists say that the Earth is 6000 years old'. Or, 'scientists say there is no evidence for evolution'

Scientists. Let me write that more correctly: 'scientists'.

There are probably tens of thousands of reputable scientists in the world and Creationists found two stupid ones with a grade 4 chemistry primer between them. These 'scientists' write with a pencil because they haven't worked out how to pop the button on an ink pen. And everyone knows that ink pens are the work of Satan.

They consult these 'scientists' for every piece of evidence that you throw at them. 'Scientists have shown *this* to be wrong.' 'Scientists have shown *that* to be wrong.' It's almost certainly the same two 'scientists' every time, running a great little business dishing out 'scientific' statements at *we-prove-science-wrong-for-cash.com*.

Every time a piece of evidence comes in and a Creationist doesn't like the look of it, they send it to these two, and they write on the bottom of it 'we say this is wrong'. And then because 'scientists' have said it's wrong, obviously it is – only a fool would question 'scientists', wouldn't he?

The Creationist tactic is to ask for evidence showing Bible inaccuracies, then rip it to pieces with some bullshit theory that their favourite 'scientists' thought up the last time they went for a shit.

Or you make a scientific point and they say, 'is *that* all you've got?' and laugh. 'Fossils? Is that all the evidence you're relying on? Hahahaha! The speed of light in a vacuum is constant? Hohohoho! Scientists say it's not!' 'Space? Scientists say it's not even there!'

In fact, I recently heard a Creationist claim that the Genesis story should not be compared with scientific evidence to see if it holds up under scrutiny, but that the process should be reversed. The gold standard for proof should be the Bible. Yes, because the Bible is the perfect word of God, if science disagrees with it, science *must* be wrong. Incredible.

I have often made the mistake of replying to someone's unscientific comments, explaining to them what the consensus of the scientific community is, and often directing them to published papers for further clarification. For every single piece of scientific evidence I quote, one Creationist or another will inevitably shoot it down with their bullshit so-called 'proof'.

It got so bad that when I talked about preparing a sample of material for testing, and I specifically mentioned putting something on a slide to see it through the microscope, this is what one of them said, and I quote:

> 'you would rather rely on a process that has to "prepare" the substance being tested in order to get the "WANTED" results before testing... and you think this is accurate???? You are naive and gullible nothing less nothing more. You do know they ALWAYS get different test results for the same exact material don't you?'

And he wasn't identifying a specific case. He meant that *every* time that *every* scientist does a test he will get different results, and that they would be wrong because he'd 'prepared' the substance before testing it.

So the simple fact that a specimen is prepared for testing is evidence that it has been tampered with to this lunatic. 'Prepared' means only 'put on a slide' or 'make sure it isn't contaminated so the results will be fair and accurate', but he thought that it meant something devious, that it was part of some kind of plot to undermine the Bible.

In another encounter, I queried the age of the Earth, as dated by the Bible. I asked: which is more accurate, the laws of nature (in this case the decay rate of different isotopes, used in radiometric dating), or an ancient book which dates the Earth by using a list of people who lived to be anything up to 900 years old, and adds them all up to get the final figure. The reply:

> All books were written by men and many are false and the Bible is the only book that hasn't been proven wrong yet.

His last word on that was: science is wrong, the Bible is right, and the Bible wins because you can't prove it's wrong.

These words should serve to warn you: if you find people like that (and there are a few around, but thankfully not too many), don't even go there. Walk away. You will achieve *nothing* by talking to them. If you're wearing a black shirt they'll swear to you that the evidence says it's white – probably because black shirts aren't in the Bible.

They are 100% closed to scientific evidence. Closed, bolted, locked, key swallowed. Nothing is going in, only bullshit is coming out. It's a road to nowhere trying to debate with someone who probably still thinks the Earth is flat and the Sun goes around it. They know a couple of 'scientists' who can prove it.

It's frustrating to find these kinds of idiots, but just be happy they are in a minority, and hope they stay that way. Conspiracy theorists have got nothing on people who think the world is 6000 years old.

And don't even get me started on the Noah's Ark story...

23

It's Just a Theory

What is a Theory?

Evolution is not a fact, it's just a theory. With that one sentence you can identify exactly which direction the conversation will go. With that single assumption, theists will sweep away vast swathes of detailed scientific research and condemn their observations, data and evidence to the toilet.

The correct definition of 'theory' is something every atheist should know, simply because the 'just a theory' argument will be thrown at you every time you mention evolution to a religious believer.

Theory: use and abuse of the word.

In everyday language, a theory can be simply described as a speculation, a hunch, or a hypothesis. If you say, 'I have a theory that when I dunk this biscuit (cookie) into my coffee it will fall in after ten seconds,' you are speculating. You may well be correct, but you did not base your speculation on evidence, so it is no more than a simple hunch.

You could, if you were so inclined, carry out scientific research[1] into biscuit dunking, and with enough experimentation could produce a body of evidence from which a more solid, equation-based description of the properties of a dunked biscuit would arise. If your

---

[1] In case you were thinking of trying it, you're too late! See the research led by Dr Len Fisher at the University of Bristol, UK, in 1998.
http://news.bbc.co.uk/1/hi/sci/tech/220400.stm

description was sufficiently robust, and always true under the same conditions, you may have succeeded in describing a scientific law.

This common use of the word 'theory' is what those who reject the Theory of Evolution mean when they say that 'evolution is just a theory'. They are under the impression that evolution is simply a hypothesis, a hunch, a guess.

They are, of course, entirely wrong. Moreover, they almost certainly already know the *actual* definition of 'theory' in science, and simply use the word incorrectly in an attempt to dismiss evolution without further debate.

To refute their nonsense, you must know your terms.

Scientific Laws.

Before looking at what the *scientific* definition of a theory is, it is useful to look at another term: a scientific law.

In simple terms, a scientific law is a 'description of behaviour'.

If you are standing on Earth and drop something such as, for example, a stone, it will fall downwards, towards the Earth. This is a simplified description of a law, in this case Sir Isaac Newton's law of universal gravitation. In more technical terms, the law was described by Newton as follows:

Every single point mass attracts every other point mass by a force heading along the line combining the two. The force is proportional to the product of the two masses and inversely proportional to the square of the magnitude between the point masses:

$$F = G \frac{m_1 m_2}{r^2}$$

Another way to look at one of the Laws of Gravity: small bodies (in terms of mass) exert less of a gravitational pull than large bodies. The moon is smaller than the Earth, so the gravitational pull at its surface is less than that of the Earth. Jupiter has much more mass than the Earth, so Jupiter exerts a much larger gravitational pull. If you 'landed' on Jupiter, the enormous forces of its gravity would crush you instantly. Indeed you yourself are a 'body' and, because you have mass, the Earth is actually being (marginally) pulled towards *you*.

Although that is a description in layman's terms, it is still covered by Newton's equations.

Most laws are conditional. They describe behaviour under certain conditions. The speed of light is 299,792,458 metres per second, a constant, but only under certain conditions. In this case the constant describes the speed of light *in a vacuum*. Light moves at lower speeds through glass or air, ie when conditions are different.

Laws are true and universal – they happen everywhere and everything must follow the law, given the same conditions. Nothing interferes with the behaviour described by the law.

The technicalities of a particular scientific law are of less importance here than the fact that laws are understood to be descriptions of behaviour. They describe absolute and inarguable facts concerning the physical world.

What a law is definitely *not* is a theory that has been proven beyond all doubt. Theories do not get 'promoted' to the status of a law once enough proof has been gathered. As I will now attempt to show, a scientific theory is a completely different concept altogether.

Scientific Theories.

If a law describes *what* happens, then a theory attempts to describe *why* it happens. The common use of the word 'theory' bears no relation to the scientific meaning of the word. To science, the word means, in its simplest terms, 'explanation'.

Newton described what happens when gravity acts on a body. His laws do not explain *why* it happens. Not at all. However, Einstein's theory of relativity *does* explain Newton's laws. Remember:

$$\text{Theory} = \text{explanation}$$

Relativity is not a subject for a short chapter in this book, but evolution is. The Theory of Evolution is one of the subjects an active, opinionated atheist must defend from Christian attack on a regular basis. The phrase 'it's just a theory' is your sign that (a) the speaker doesn't know a thing about evolution or (b) dogmatically refuses to accept that a scientific theory is much more than a theory in the non-scientific ('hypothesis') sense.

A scientific theory describes the behaviour of natural phenomena. It must be rigorously tested, confirmed by experimentation and observation, and supported by data. As well as describing existing data, it must make predictions, which must also be testable.

A theory must have conditions that, if met, would prove the theory wrong. For example, if identifiable human fossils were found in exactly the same rock strata as, say, a Tyrannosaurus rex, the theory of evolution would almost certainly be in serious doubt. So attempts to disprove evolution, and other theories, must be successfully survived.

This means that everything to which science gives the title 'theory' is already well supported by evidence. A theory is not 'just' a theory at all. It describes *facts*. It *explains* facts.

Evolution is a fact. Evolution happens and is happening. The *Theory* of Evolution describes *why* it happens. Even if the theory never existed, or if it was shown to be wrong, evolution would still be a fact. In that case we would simply not know why evolution happened, but we would still know for a fact that it did.

Just as if we were unable to explain gravity, that would not stop objects falling to the ground – gravity would still be a fact.

Evolution being the controversial subject that it is, it has managed to survive more attacks on its integrity than perhaps all the other scientific theories combined. This also means that there is an incredible amount of data to support evolution. It has survived all attempts be proven incorrect, the mark of any good scientific theory, and stands alone as the accepted explanation for the development of complex life on Earth.

To further dismiss the notion that it is 'just a theory', let's remember the definition of 'theory', which is 'explanation'. What then does the theory of evolution explain? The Theory of Evolution explains evolution. That is an important point. Evolution *is* a series of facts. The theory merely explains how evolution works. Without saying 'proof', which we can never do, a scientific theory is as close as we can ever come to a position where evolution is what we would call truth.

Proof.

Is the Theory of Evolution proven? The answer is: no.
Hmm.

This would seem to be a weakness in our argument with Creationists. If evolution is not proven, then there is no proof that evolution is true.

Not exactly.

No scientific theory can be called 'proven'. If you perform an experiment a million times and get the same results each time, you can be confident that the next time you conduct the experiment you will get the same results. But you can never be absolutely certain. Never.

If even a single experiment or observation disproves the Theory of Evolution, the whole theory will fall. So far this has not happened, but you could do every experiment every day, an endless number of times, and it is still possible that the *next* experiment would disprove the theory.

So no theory is ever true. Take electromagnetic theory, which describes the behaviour of electric and magnetic fields, and how they interact with matter. This is a theory. It has never been disproved, and there is no expectation that it will be, but it *is* possible.

When was the last time you heard a Creationist saying that electromagnetic theory is 'just a theory'? What about cell theory? Atomic theory? Christian 'science' accepts other theories without question. Only Evolution Theory and Big Bang Theory are brought up by Creationists as being 'just theories'.

To a Christian, evolution and the Big Bang (the science of the origins of the Universe) are things he cannot accept because the consequences for his religion are far too damaging to consider. If evolution is correct, the Bible is wrong. There is no middle ground here. If man was created by God on the sixth day, evolution never happened. If evolution is correct, God did not create the animals at all.

So Creationists claim that evolution is 'just a theory'. What they are trying to have you believe is that science considers evolution as 'just a hunch'. This is absolutely not the case. The Theory of Evolution is one of the most researched fields of study in history, accepted by every reputable scientific organisation on the planet, and it has yet to be disproved. Science has evidence. Creationists simply deny the evidence.

God as a Scientific Theory.

Christians claim to 'know' that God is real. They have proof. It's all in the Bible. The Bible is the true and perfect word of God. Christians want Intelligent Design (which is really Creationism) taught in schools alongside evolution, as an alternative theory.

Although the 'designer' is not named, they of course mean 'God'. But 'God exists' is not a scientific theory. Intelligent Design is not a scientific theory. There is no evidence, no data; there are no experiments that can be done to show that supernatural forces were responsible for life on Earth.

ID gives no predictions, no way to verify any of its claims. Importantly, it can never be proven wrong. It therefore cannot be described as a scientific theory at all.

Christians leap up and down with glee, knowing that science cannot disprove God. I deal with our inability to disprove God elsewhere in this book, but let me add: I cannot disprove fairies, and there is as much credible evidence for fairies as there is for the existence of God – none at all.

But let's be generous here. Let's say that God is 1% proven. And let's be unkind to science and say that evolution is only 90% proven. Which is the better choice? Why believe in something which is as unlikely to be true as 1%, when the 90% choice is a much safer 'bet'?

Of course these percentages are incorrect. The solid, undeniable facts which would prove the existence of God simply do not exist. So we are looking at something approaching 0%. Science's proofs are much more rigorously enforced before a theory can be accepted. We are looking at 99.99% proof for evolution. Why believe in something which has no chance of being correct, rather than something which has every chance of being correct?

But Christians will say they are 100% certain that God exists, and they know this despite having absolutely no proof whatsoever. Why do they believe, despite a total lack of evidence, and in the face of a huge amount of evidence to the contrary? Your guess is as good as mine.

Terms of Reference.

You should look at these terms of reference again, just to make sure you have a good grasp of the basic concepts. You will undoubtedly need them if you ever choose to debate science with a Christian.

    Theory   - Guess, hunch, hypothesis (common use)
    Scientific Law   - Description of behaviour
    Scientific Theory - Explanation of facts

A law is *what*, a theory is *why*.

And Creation 'science' or Intelligent Design? They are nonsense.

24

After-Life Comparisons

Double heathen burger and fries please.

As you'll know by now, I do not believe that there is a God, or any other supernatural being in the Universe. I have no respect for religion, and this book is all about showing you that it is genuinely okay for you to hold such an opinion. Someone's choice of religion deserves no more reverence than their choice of breakfast cereal.

However, a big part of the real dislike and resentment I have for Christianity in particular is the teaching of eternal damnation for everyone in the world who doesn't repent and follow Jesus Christ. Christianity teaches that all atheists like me will go to Hell, along with all Jews, Muslims, Buddhists, Hindus, Sikhs, and everyone else who isn't a Christian.

It's actually worse than that because there are plenty of Christians out there (remember, E is for Evangelist) who consider that only they are 'true' Christians. Even other Christians, who of course aren't really Christians because they don't tick all the Fundie boxes, aren't going to Heaven.

Remember that Hell will be eternal. You will burn forever in a lake of fire, becoming crispier by the day, and presumably your body will be indestructible so you'll never be put out of your misery. Or maybe you'll be turned to ashes, given a new body and start over. Ahh, now I understand – if you're not born again, you'll end up burned again.

So it's going to hurt. A lot. And the pain isn't going to end. Unlike Oprah you can't turn it off when the torture becomes unbearable.

The only way you can get to Heaven if Christianity is right is by repenting your sins and giving your life to Jesus.

I don't want to be picky, but this really narrows it down a lot doesn't it? But hey, so what? If you don't believe it, don't let it bother you, right?

What bothers me is that parents tell their *children* these lies. Where do you think the expression 'put the fear of God into them' comes from? Making children fearful of some imaginary super-being in the clouds is as wrong as threatening to cut off their ears if they misbehave. It's mental abuse, and if we're talking about children, that is the worst abuse I can think of.

And to my mind it's all crap. If there is a God (and I don't believe there is), would he really want all the Muslims to go to Hell if they do actually believe in him but in a different way?

Or the Jews. The Jews have had some real shit all through history (not entirely unconnected to persecution by Christians), but they do believe in God, and they're assuming that God is probably pretty pleased about that.

Peace and confusion.

Unfortunately when Christ showed up, this messed it up for the Jews. Big time. Now unless the Jews believe JC is their saviour they are all going to Hell. And naturally they don't believe this, so the Jews are going to burn, according to Christianity.

But all religions are just as bad as Christianity for this, right?

Let's take a look at the Jewish faith. No in-depth analysis, just a basic comparison.

Similarities first:

Christians and Jews believe in God.

And that's about it. There are very few similarities other than the Ten Commandments.

Differences:

For Jews, Jesus was not the Messiah. That's because the Messiah is a human who will bring peace to the world. So if Jesus was the Messiah, did he bring peace? Out of 100 people taking part in the Crusades or the Inquisition, and a sample from every century since year 1, our survey said that zero agreed with the statement 'there is peace in the world'. There has *never* been a time in recorded history when the whole of the world has been at peace. It just didn't happen. And don't expect it to happen in your lifetime.

Jews don't believe that Jesus was the son of God. For Jews there is no god but God, and that's true for Muslims too – to become a Muslim you start by saying 'There is no god but Allah'.

Jews don't believe in the three parts of God – the Father, the Son and the Holy Spirit. And I have to say, Christians, you're making a piss poor job of explaining that particular three-in-one ensemble to everyone, including your own followers. God is his own son, so he's his own father too, and there's this other spirit thing that nobody has seen, and they're all the same but different, and God sent down his son but that was really himself. Okaaaaay…

For the Jews there's just one God, one creator of everything. And for atheists that makes it easy – we don't believe in the Jewish God either.

Christians condemn everyone to the fire.

Okay, so here's where it becomes really interesting, and where Christianity shows its true colours and demonstrates how much of an intolerant and bigoted religion it really is.

For Christians, everyone is born into sin. Everyone. People are bad right from birth. Babies? Bad. Still in the womb? Bad. A 150-cell embryo? Bad. That's smaller than the dot on this 'i' but Christian doctrine says it has a soul, so it must be sinful.

Any person, even a child, who has not 'accepted Christ into their heart' is, in Christian philosophy, a rotten, vile, disgusting sinner who deserves to go to Hell, even for the slightest wrongdoing. There is no grey area here. This is Christian doctrine. This is what Christianity teaches.

The only way you can get to Heaven is through Jesus, for which you have to repent and be born again. So you don't get a chance to even start out good. Right from day one you're assumed to be a sinner. You naughty foetus you!

On the other hand, Jews believe that humans aren't born bad, and they aren't born good. Everyone has free will, and the ability to choose an ethical life for themselves. So humans aren't damned to Hell before they've even started, Jews believe that everyone has a clean slate.

What the Jewish faith focuses on is leading a good life while you're alive, and then thinking about death and the after-life when it's nearer the time.

Here's the important part for me, and it's about what the Jewish faith believes will happen to people when they die. The very first chapter of this book, which is called 'Serve God or Burn Forever', notes that Christianity preaches torture for the majority of the people on the planet. Most people are going to burn in the lake of fire, and it will be never-ending. Don't expect to go water-skiing when you get there.

However, the Jewish faith's view of life after death is totally different. It's much more liberal. It describes a God who loves *everybody*, even if they aren't Jewish.

Judaism doesn't believe you'll automatically go to Hell if you're not a Jew. It also doesn't believe you'll automatically go to Heaven if you *are* a Jew. It's your behaviour that's important, how you live your life.

It's all the things that make absolutely no difference to Christians if you're not a believer. To a Christian, even if you live a well-behaved, ethical, moral life, but you're not a Christian, you're still going to Hell, to burn forever, blah blah blah etc.

So to Judaism, everyone who is good will be rewarded, whoever they are, and even if you're not good, punishment isn't eternal.

For Jews, the afterlife is like the ultimate justice system, where you pay the price according to what you've done in life. Once you've paid that price, paid for any bad things you did in your life, that's it. You're not going to burn *forever* just for not believing in God.

Obviously if Heaven and Hell exist but you don't believe in them, with Christianity you've had it – you'll be in Hell, and although when you're in Hell you're obviously going to start believing in God pretty damned quick, it's tough luck. Too late, no way out – you burn.

If you're Jewish, you have the chance to make good for anything you've done on Earth. There's acceptance for everyone, and any punishment (if there is one) isn't going to last forever. The punishment fits the crime, and no more than that.

All for Hell and Hell for all.

For Christianity, one punishment fits all. Child rapist? Burn in Hell. Jewish rabbi? Burn in Hell. Pious Catholic monk? The Evangelists say you will burn in Hell too. For Catholic monks that's probably true anyway, because they really shouldn't be reading this book!

You can see why I think Christianity is one of the worst religions we have. Certainly it's in the top two with Islam. If I believed in God I'd want him to be like the Jewish interpretation of God – a God who forgives everyone, and doesn't torment you in Hell forever just because you were born in the wrong country and adopted the wrong religion.

In the past when I've told Christians that I'd want God to be this way, if I believed in him, they said it wasn't up to me to decide how God behaved. But why not? Man invented religion, why should my interpretation of what God should be be any less valid? It's not is if all Christians believe the same thing is it? Why, when I think of Protestants and Catholics, do I always hear a voice inside my head saying, 'Let's get ready to rumblllllle'?

Obviously the important thing is that I am an atheist. I don't believe in God *at all*. And yet although all religions are simply mindless delusions to me, I get the impression that Judaism is at least making the effort to be inclusive rather than divisive.

And the good thing is, with the Jewish God good atheists get rewarded too, so Pascal's Wager is meaningless – everybody wins!

If you're going to worship God, just do it, and don't bother me. As soon as you tell me I will be tortured unless I convert, I just add you to the 'intolerant git' list.

Even a superficially inclusive religion such as Judaism is still fundamentally a fairy tale, a myth-based fantasy. Jews worship the invisible man in the sky, as do Christians and Muslims. And if you look into its customs, Judaism, like all other religions, has its darker aspects which its modern followers are keen to play down.

This was *not* a message of support for Judaism.

A comparison such as this simply highlights the madness that is religion. You can believe in the same God, but one set of people will believe he is a mad psycho who rains down vengeance on those who don't worship him, and another set of people will believe… that he is a mad psycho who rains down vengeance on those who don't worship him.

Well have you *read* the Old Testament?

In Cash We Trust

The evolution of the currency.

Since their first appearance in 1864, the words 'In God We Trust' have been stamped on some US coins, though not all, and not continuously. In 1955 a law was passed which made it mandatory for *all* US coinage and paper currency to show 'In God We Trust'.

Prior to 1956, and in fact dating from the American Revolution in the 18th century, the national motto of the United States was 'E Pluribus Unum' (out of many, one), but 1956 saw religion stamp its mark and over-rule history and tradition. An act of Congress was passed which made 'In God We Trust' the official national motto of the US. Although both the old and new mottoes are to be found on all US coins, and on the one dollar bill, 'In God We Trust' is everywhere.

American atheists don't like this. Since they don't believe there is a God, they certainly don't trust in God, not at all. Separation of church and state, embodied in the US Constitution's First Amendment, should, opponents argue, require that any such motto be removed. However, all legal attempts to do so have so far failed.

In the UK, we have the letters 'FD', or sometimes 'FID DEF', printed on all our coins, both of which are abbreviations for the Latin 'Fidei Defensor', or 'Defender of the Faith'. The UK's history is much different, of course, and we have an official state religion, the Church of England, though you wouldn't know it – church attendance is very low, around the 5% mark.

Our notes show different characters from British history. Elizabeth Fry (a social reformer) is on the £5 note. Composer Sir Edward Elgar is on the £20. The relatively unknown Sir John Houblon ended up on the £50 for no other reason than he was the first Governor of the Bank of England.

But there's one note I've missed, the £10 note, and I single it out for reasons which will be obvious. Again, it shows a famous British historical figure, this time a man who lived from 1809 to 1882. He was a country gentleman, but also a man of science and travelled widely. He is someone who will be very familiar to you.

Charles Darwin.

There he is, on the back of our £10 note. Clearly and unashamedly it is Charles Darwin. Now imagine how the news would be received in churches across America if Congress passed a law requiring Darwin's picture to be added to the currency, presumably under the excellent motto 'In Science We Trust'. Another Civil War, anyone?

Take it off.

No atheists want 'In God We Trust' on US currency. At best they may be indifferent, but in general there is a feeling that it would be better if it were removed. It is divisive. It ignores the lives of a large section of Americans who genuinely do *not* trust in God.

Christians, meanwhile, try to assure atheists that they should not be offended by four words. But how laid back would they be if those four words were 'There Is No God'? Imagine the protests of millions of Christians in the streets if any hint of this happening became likely, and perhaps a similarly strong reaction if the US Government hinted that 'In God We Trust' might be removed.

And what if the currency said, 'In Allah We Trust'?

'In God We Trust' is an imposition of religion where it isn't wanted. But it's the law. Separation of church and state means nothing when to simply live your life in America you *have* to carry money with a religious motto printed on it.

But every time I pull out a £10 note it brings a smile to my face. The UK celebrates that great man of Evolutionary Theory, Charles Darwin. It's clear that in my country, despite our official state religion, we trust in science, not God.

26

Fallacies, Lies, Strawmen and Dogma

The empty Christian mind.

Sometimes you'll find a Christian whose every word shows so much ignorance of what he is attempting to refute that it is genuinely breathtaking. These are people whose 'arguments' you will find easy to refute. You need only a simple list of points, and a knowledge of some basic science, to prove them wrong. The more you know, the more obvious it will become that your opponent knows practically nothing.

This chapter gives a summary of such statements, all of them commonly put forward by ignorant Christians.

Evolution is a religion.

Wrong. A religion requires faith. Faith is 'belief that does not rest on logical proof or material evidence'. Evolution is based on a *vast* amount of evidence. And nobody prays to any god of evolution when they want to increase their chances of winning the lottery.

Evolution says we come from nowhere.

Evolution is a working description of a process of nature. It explains how diverse life forms developed from early life. For evolution to happen, life must already exist. Evolution says nothing about the origin of life. Nothing.

The origin of life is described in a scientific model, known as abiogenesis. As with 'atheist' we can break down this word, which has Greek origins: a-bio-genesis means 'without biological origins', or to put it another way, 'life from no life'. Even if there was a God (also without biological origins!) who was himself the creator of life, evolution would not be involved in it, makes no mention of it, and would still be valid whatever the origins of the *first* life.

The Theory of Evolution isn't a scientific theory.

This book devotes a whole chapter to the definition of theories and laws, as understood by science. Evolution *is* a scientific theory. It is an explanation of facts. A *vast* array of facts. It has yet to be contradicted and proven wrong, but as with all scientific theories remains open to the possibility of refinement and change.

Evolution contradicts the Second Law of Thermodynamics.

The SLT states that 'the entropy of an isolated system not in equilibrium will tend to increase over time, approaching a maximum value at equilibrium.' Or, more simply, 'heat cannot of itself pass from a colder to a hotter body.'

A simple example would be: ice melts in a warm room. The heat energy gained by the ice from the room, which causes it to melt, will not be lost back into the room if that room is warmer – the ice will not re-form. The equilibrium here is room temperature.

The key phrase you need to remember here is 'isolated system' or 'closed system'. What Creationists are suggesting is that complex life cannot arise from simple life. But the Earth is *not* a closed system. It orbits the Sun, which provides it with a vast amount of new energy. To take the ice example, 'of itself' the water could not change back to ice, but there are many ways you *could* make ice – the fridge in your kitchen takes energy from an outside source and does exactly that.

Evolution says that man evolved from monkeys.

It says no such thing. Evolution says that primates (monkeys and apes) and man evolved from a common ancestor, some time in the past. As such, we are not direct descendants, but we are related. Think of monkeys and apes as our cousins.

Monkeys are better adapted to their environment.

Yes, they are, because it is *their* environment. You don't see monkeys living with penguins, simply because penguins have evolved to be able to adapt to the cold. Monkeys do not live there, because they evolved to suit different conditions, elsewhere in the world. Humans are found in a wide range of environments because our brains have evolved to a point where we have been able to develop clothing, tools and technology to allow us to do so. But put a human in the environment of an ape, without clothing or tools, and we would struggle to survive because our evolution has taken a different path. We are poorly adapted to some environments.

We are no more or less evolved than any other animal. All species alive today have evolved by natural selection to adapt to their environment. In that sense, animals and humans really are all equal.

There is no missing link between monkeys and humans.

Examine the fossil evidence. There are many intermediate species known to exist which demonstrate the path that evolution took from a common ancestor to present-day human. Other primates simply took a different path, and they are different branches on the evolutionary 'tree'.

Chromosome 2.

You won't hear any mention of chromosome 2 from Creationists because it is devastating to their case. Humans have 23 pairs of chromosomes, but primates have 24 pairs. Why would we have less than our ape cousins? Examination of chromosome 2 shows that, somewhere in our evolutionary history, two pairs of chromosomes fused together. We can prove this by looking at the chromosomes in primates, and in humans, which show solid evidence that this occurred.

Think of it something like this: if you bake two cookies next to each other in the oven, they may spread out in the process, and merge together. While this 'double cookie' is certainly still a cookie, you can examine it for evidence which suggests that it was formed from two separate cookies. This is the case with chromosome 2, formed from the fusion of two pairs of chromosomes.

Don't expect this cookie analogy to be accepted by a seasoned debater of course – you will need to use the terms 'vestigial centromere' and 'vestigial telomere', which will require further reading. This is research and knowledge which the Creationist simply will not do – if he is already telling you that man evolved from monkeys, you can safely assume he knows next to nothing about evolution in general.

98% of our DNA is shared with apes.
99% of our DNA is shared with mice.

This is correct. But DNA is a common component of *all* life. We have many things in common with a wide variety of animals. This argument leads nowhere – a valid reply would be: 'so what?'. Is the speaker suggesting that mice evolved from apes, and then we evolved from mice? We have two eyes, and so does a salmon, but this does not mean that we evolved directly from a fish.

Dinosaurs and man co-existed.

Oh dear. Now we are roaming deep into fantasy land. The evidence that Christians have for 'man walking with dinosaurs' has been discredited for decades, and consists of human footprints supposedly found in the same strata as fossil dinosaur prints. Search for a reference to 'Paluxy River tracks' and you will find evidence of deliberately misinterpreted data and downright forgery. The fraud is well documented, but is still touted by some Creationists as 'proof' that dinosaurs and man co-existed. By comparison, the Piltdown Man, exposed as a hoax long ago, is *never* used by scientists to prove their case... but Creationists won't let science forget it of course!

The difference here is that science learns from its mistakes. Religion covers them up, ignores them, or, sometimes, just keeps right on making the same mistakes again and again. Ignorance and a closed mind are both symptoms of religious delusion.

Importantly, none of the hoaxes held up by Creationists to discredit science actually go any way at all towards *disproving* the vast amount of valid scientific evidence still available. They are simply no longer examples of evidence *for* the case.

Reptiles only appear in the 'reptile layer'.

This refers to the fact that, as species evolved, certain types of animals appear at different times in the 'geologic column' (the layers of rock, or strata, in which fossils are found). If someone says that reptiles, for example, are only found in the 'reptile layer', and that birds are only found in the 'bird layer', they are wrong.

The layers shown in text books show where types of animals *first* appeared. So fish are found low in the column, but once they appear, they are found all the way up to the present day. Reptiles appear later, but when they appear they are found in all strata to the present, as are fish. When birds appear, we find birds *and* fish *and* reptiles.

The Noah's Ark story explains the fossil record.

Creationists believe that the Great Flood killed all life except eight people and a boat full of animals. Fossils are found in order in different strata because (and you may need to sit down for this) simple animals sank to the bottom very quickly, but lizards, amphibians and dinosaurs floated in the water a bit longer before they sank too. Mammals, birds and humans all managed to float even longer, before they too sank and became fossils. All this happened in a single year, sometime around 2500 BC.

Need I go on to say why this is bullshit?

There are dozens of ways to refute this ludicrous idea, the best of which, simple common sense, should be your tool of choice. However, my favourite is the fact that fossil dinosaur footprints are found only in strata where those dinosaurs are also found. How then did the footprint sink through the flood waters at the same rate as the matching dinosaur?

We have stopped evolving.

Not true. For example, average human height in the West has increased by several inches in the last 100 years. Medical advances yes, better food yes, but these simply mirror, and accelerate, the natural processes used by animals who find better food and living conditions by foraging and adapting to their environment. Certainly we have reduced some areas of natural selection – spectacles reduce the need for perfect vision, and some illnesses now have cures where previously nature would 'select' only those who were resistant to disease – but there is no denying that life continues to evolve.

When Europeans first visited the Americas, they took with them many diseases against which the European physiology had already developed resistance. The native populations of the Americas were devastated by disease, but those which had resistance managed to survive. This is natural selection. As surely as insects develop resistance to pesticides, populations of humans develop resistance to disease.

There is some evidence that Christians have stopped evolving, and in fact that evolution is in reverse, but it would be wrong to base this hypothesis on science!

Why are there still apes?
Why didn't everything evolve into humans?

Again this shows a lack of understanding of evolution. Evolution describes the way in which a *diversity* of life has appeared. Each species has adapted to suit different environments. Humans live near rivers, but they don't live *in* rivers, so fish are better adapted, even though they live nearby. Frogs prefer still pools rather than fast-running water, but some fish can live in both – neither one is 'more' evolved, they are simply better suited to different environments. This applies to apes as much as it applies to any other species on the planet.

Evolution is just random chance.
How can an eye just appear by chance?

This is probably the biggest misconception of all about evolution. However, I will resist the temptation to explain why these statements are wrong, and instead invite you to do your own research into evolutionary processes. If you don't know why something happens, and why evolution is far from being 'just chance'… find out!

Do your own research.

Research is what everyone, atheists or otherwise, should be prepared to undertake whenever they are challenged to discuss a subject and find that they have gaps in their knowledge. There is no shame in saying 'I do not know' and then going to find out. This is the essence of education, and striving to learn more is a tremendously positive attitude to adopt.

What Creationists are saying is, 'We refuse to believe any explanation which is not Biblical'. Science is closed to a mind such as this. A well-rounded education, feeding an inquiring mind, is not something these people will ever strive to obtain. Instead, it is replaced by the single-minded, unwaveringly belief that 'the word of God', as written in the Bible, is correct. Nothing and no one, not even a wide-ranging body of knowledge accumulated over hundreds of years of research, will come between the dogmatic believer and their precious Bronze Age mythology.

In reality, if you find yourself talking to someone whose views include some of the misplaced statements found in this chapter, simply walk away and don't waste your time arguing. They probably don't even want to listen to what you have to say. They certainly won't believe that your knowledge of science puts any doubt on the 'truth' of the one ancient book they (may) have been willing to read.

God Almighty's Genesis Diary – Day 4

Day 4 – Thursday

9:10 am

I forgot to mention that The Holy Spirit did me a big favour and worked the night shift last night, just to make sure the plants would stay put. Did I say 'favour'? Turns out that all the lazy bastard wanted was a boozy night around the campfire with his buddies.

So what do I find this morning? Beer cans, smouldering trees and a big slick of engine oil from their quad bikes, that's what. Some of those plants cost me serious money, and by my reckoning I've lost three, maybe four thousand species already. All because dick-wad couldn't be bothered to make his own heat.

Does he have his own powers? Yes. Does he bother working up a sweat to use them? Of course not. He just fires a thunderbolt out of his scrawny ass and burns my damned forest.

So now on top of all the other shit I've had this week, I have to install some security lighting to make sure it doesn't happen again.

9:30 am

Started making two lights, one for the day and one for the night. Yeah we already had light, but these babies really brighten up the place. He can run but he can't hide.

The Holy Spirit and his idiot friends won't dare try anything now. If they so much as look at one of my forests I will execute great vengeance upon them with furious rebukes. And they shall know that I am the Lord, when I shall lay my vengeance upon them.

In fact I'll kick their scrawny butts into the middle of next week if I catch them.

10:45 am

He called me. He's sorry. Yeah right. Whatever. I gave him one hour to clean the mess up, and although he said he was onto it (something about burying it and calling it coal), I'll believe it when I see it. You can't believe a word the Holy Spirit says – I've got no faith in the guy.

12:20 pm

My Sun and Moon are just about ready, and the Sun in particular seems to be perking up the vegetation. That's a side effect I hadn't anticipated, but if it helps them grow that's less work for me. I just need to glue both of them in place, so protective gloves on and here we go.

There's probably time for a beer or five while the glue dries. Cool.

1:30 pm

Remember my 'let there be light, or dirt, or whatever' thing? Well, I shouldn't really mention it but there's this big red button marked 'Make It So' on my desk and that sort of takes care of it. Technically I have all the power I need, but the button is what it all comes down to.

So you know how it is, after a liquid lunch at the bar across the road from the main office, I've got an idea. The job title is 'Lord God Almighty', so almighty it's going to be.

All I need to do is press the button down permanently and then everything I say will come to pass. It will be like I really am all-powerful. Let there be mountains. Zap. Let there be, I dunno, flying metal discs all around the Universe. Zap.

I think I said that last one out loud. Oops. Nobody will notice.

This is going to be great. Time to strut my stuff and show what a real God is made of.

1:45 pm

Damn kids. While I was out to lunch some of the little bastards from the estate have only gone and put my Earth in orbit around the Sun. It's supposed to be the other way around!

1:50 pm

It's worse. They dunked my lovely Moon into the sea and put the fire out altogether. It looks like they've been kicking it around, judging by all the dents and craters in it, and the thing is a total write-off now.

I wish I had a billion of these Suns, then they'd find out if anyone can hear you scream in space. I'd make sure the little bastards never played with my stuff again.

2:30 pm

Yeah you know that thing with the button? I think I worked out why nobody keeps it pressed down. See, I don't actually have to say 'let there be a billion Suns', because technically 'I wish' means the same thing. Where the fuck am I going to put all these things?

2:50 pm

Space is big. Thank... well, be thankful anyway. So I just threw all the stars into it and to be honest I think I've made the best out of a bad job. They look kind of pretty anyway. There were a few duds, but I just rolled up the innards, gave them a lick of paint, and I'm going to call them planets.

4:20 pm

There's all kinds of bangs going on in the Universe. I think some of my stars (for administration purposes I had to give them a new name) have collided or something. Remind me not to drink on the job again. This day has been a nightmare, and the noise has given me a headache.

4:45 pm

A couple of the Laws of Science turned up, to let me know they've caught the kids responsible for dunking my Moon, and do I want to press charges? They seemed to be upset when I suggested that I would burn the little buggers for all eternity if I caught them, and warned me not to take any of the Laws into my own hands.

They also mentioned something about a stolen sleigh which had been found abandoned and vandalised a couple of days ago. Of course I said that was nothing to do with me, but they gave me that look and said they might have to ask me a few more questions at some point.

Note to self: when Laws of Science start asking awkward questions, remember to always have a good excuse. They can't prove anything.

The Holy Threesome

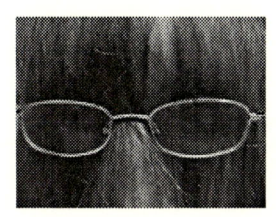

And after the supper there was a second cup, filled with lemonade. For many would be driving their donkeys later and Jesus had brought a non-alcoholic option. Yet they drank it not when he told them, This is my pee-pee.

The Last Supper But One

Cheesy Jesus.

Greetings. I am the wise man of the woods. Yes, it's me again.
   My back is much better now. Thank you for asking. But my elbow is giving me a bit of trouble. I have the wise-man's elbow, which comes from beating 50 Christians with branches every day. They seem to like it, and they pay me well, no questions asked. I buy little ornaments for my cave, and the occasional pack of the Budweiser.

I bring you knowledge. That is my job.

But first I must ask you one question.

Mankind has invented many crazy stories about the three Christian God parts. We know of the God, and of the Jesus... but the Holy Spirit keeps himself very secretive. Yet in the story of the three bears we hear of all three of these furry creatures, with their yummy porridge and their comfy beds.

The question you must consider is this:

Does the Holy Spirit stay hidden because he has a personal hygiene problem?

I will give you a moment to think about it.

Are you thinking?

Your moment is over.

The answer to this question can be found only in the sacred book of Willis. For it is written:

And in those times there were many false religions, and those which were most false were truly those with names of great length. So it was that Christianity thought itself most important because it beat Judaism 5 syllables to 4.

And in those days there came Islam. But the older religions scorned it, saying, 'Take thee hence, oh bearded ones, thy syllables are small in number.' And Islam made haste, but came back with many metal birds to silence those who mocked its syllabic deficiency.

Yet still, a storm was raging. But it cleared up for the weekend, with some sunny intervals in the west.

There came a new religion, which spake not its name but declared its syllables to be without number. Thrice did Christianity call it out, and thrice was it defiant. But Jesus walked in the land of these people, and discovered that its name was long, and yea, it was pretentious, and the people did believe that someone had just made it up.

And accursed was this name, for it was: Zoroastrianism.

And the many religions with their shorter names knew that this was just taking the piss, and they beat Zoroastrianism about the head with burning bushes, baskets of bread and fish, and some kosher beef burgers – only 5% fat. Mmm, tasty.

Thus spake the book of Willis, for the book of Willis knows what it is talking about.

Thereafter, Zoroastrianism was forced to hide in a cupboard, and became an alcoholic. It is from his love of malt whisky that the name 'Holy Spirit' was given to him.

So the answer to the question is this: the Holy Spirit *does* have a personal hygiene problem. But, he is in rehab and should be home by Tuesday.

The wise man must now go, but he will return. He is opening a new Tesco supermarket in Wigan on the 15th. First 50 customers get a free chicken. So be early because every little helps.

Killing for Atheism

Remember Communism?

Christians have, throughout history, persecuted other religions. The Crusades and the Inquisition are the most visible evidence of the Holy Wars against Jews and Muslims, but there are many other examples.

If you bring up that point with a Christian, chances are you'll get the names Stalin, Mao and Pol Pot thrown back at you, as examples of atheists who ruthlessly persecuted the religious communities of their countries. Millions died because of their actions. And, yes, they were atheists.

But they were also socialists, Marxists, and, most important of all, communists. Karl Marx himself said that atheism 'has no longer any meaning' and 'socialism as such no longer needs this mediation'.

These three men were therefore following a political system in which atheism was *meaningless*. It was not the prime motivation for their actions.

Communism teaches that individual property ownership is evil. Religions, by their very nature, gather in places of worship, often at the largest and most conspicuous landmark in their town or village. They have property, money and influence in the communities they serve. Communism specifically demands that such power and possessions be taken away.

Communism also rejects the hierarchy of the class system, while religion embodies such a hierarchical system. Again, it is no surprise that organised religion was a prime target for communist dictators.

But we should recognise that in their time these men removed *all* obstructions in their path, not merely religious ones. It was communism, not atheism, which was their prime motivation.

Stalin, Mao and Pol Pot possessed a complete hatred of anyone opposed to their communist ideals. Those who dared to challenge communism were simply removed.

They were atheists, certainly, but like most atheists this fact meant little to them. That they did not believe in God was something they had in common, but equally all three men had dark hair. Nobody is suggesting that hair colour fuelled their genocidal tendencies.

The driving force for their persecution of religion was communism. It was also the driving force for their persecution of all land-owners, political opponents, intellectuals, and dissenters. Their motivation was not atheism, it was communism.

Always remember that atheism is an absence of belief in any god. The reason that atheists are hard to categorise is that an absence of something is not easily defined. I have an absence of purple shirts in my wardrobe, but that doesn't mean I have much in common with you if this is something you 'share' with me. If I ever commit a crime, it is to be hoped you would not believe that I am some kind of despicable a-purplist.

This extreme form of communism no longer exists in the world, even in China where communism is still in power. We should not deny that Stalin, Mao and Pol Pot were evil, genocidal, power-hungry dictators. Nor should we lie about their atheism. But their despicable actions were motivated by communism, not by atheism. The very founder of communism, Karl Marx, rejected the need for atheism.

We should not be overly concerned that Christians point to Stalin, Mao and Pol Pot as being examples of 'evil atheists', any more than these three men were 'evil non-blondes'. What motivates the actions of these killers, the root cause of their behaviour, what drove them to execute millions of people, was a misguided but absolute belief in a political system called communism.

Comparing Christianity to Racism

Racists vs Anti-racists.

Why do atheists bother speaking out against Christianity? Why have I spent several months making atheist videos for YouTube? Why are many others doing so now, some far more prolifically than I ever did? Why am I writing this book, a book about atheism to be read by atheists, who surely don't need much convincing that there is no God?

Why would someone who has no belief in the existence of something, whatever it is, spend any time at all even thinking about it, much less preparing an argument and speaking out against it?

Many people believe in ghosts. I have no belief ghosts. I do not believe there are such things as ghosts, spectres, poltergeists, ghouls or any other bedsheet-based life forms. Why then do I not make videos rebutting the arguments of the ghost believers? Why am I not determinedly a-spookist?

Consider religion in the same way that you would think of racism.

Some people believe that one race is superior to another. Many, hopefully most, people do not. However most people who have no racist tendencies at all never speak about their absence of racism. Perhaps it never comes up, or perhaps racism does not impact on their lives. Perhaps they are part of a family of racists who, although their ideas are wrong, would be upset if a family member stood up against them. Or perhaps they are simply not the kind of person who likes to speak up and protest. There are all kinds of people in the world, after all.

But there are some people who will speak out against racism. They will not tolerate racist language. If they hear it they will start an argument rather than let it go by. They may join anti-racist marches and protests. They may even make videos, write articles or books, or speak out in public against racist ideas.

These people have no belief in racism, and in fact they hold the opposite viewpoint. Though there is no such word, they are active, or strong, a-racists.

They will direct their fiercest anti-racist sentiments at those people who are openly racist. The people who are doing most harm are those who actively practice racism, therefore it is those people at whom the anti-racists will direct their attention.

Christians vs Atheists.

Many people believe in the teachings of the Bible. They believe in God and Jesus Christ. These are Christians. Those who have no belief in the Christian God, or any other god, are atheists. Most atheists simply have no belief in God and their atheism goes no further than that. This non-entity, this absence of belief, is like a non-belief in pixies; they see little point in speaking out because they have no interest in doing so. There would be no point.

However, some atheists actively speak out, both for atheist ideals, and against Christian teachings. For many atheists Christianity does impact on their lives. When devout Christians become elected officials and begin to make laws which discriminate against non-Christians, atheists speak out. When Christians say that science is wrong about evolution, or that the Earth is only 6000 years old, atheists know that this is wrong, and some of them speak out. When atheists see religious leaders trying to promote the teaching of Intelligent Design (Creationism by another name) in schools, some of them, perhaps parents of children at the schools who will be affected, will want to speak out.

Active, or strong atheism, is as valid a protest as any other. As surely as a person can be an active racist or an active anti-racist, people can be active Christians or active atheists. Some atheists join organisations, forming pressure groups to protest against particular issues, or discussing the philosophy, politics or science behind specific religious topics.

Many atheists feel as strongly about religion as those who are anti-racist. They feel the need to share their views and get the message out there. Religion is not like the Easter Bunny – there are no politicians being elected on the strength of their lop-eared rabbit policies. Religion is political, so atheists must be political to combat it. Religion influences many areas of everyday life, so atheists try to show that these influences can often be damaging.

I do not believe in the Hindu gods and yet I do not speak out about Hinduism. Why? Because I do not come into contact with many Hindus, they do not regularly tell me I am going to burn in Hell, they don't call science into doubt, they don't get elected into my country's government and try to pass laws which have a negative impact on my life. I have no reason to speak against the Hindu religion.

Christianity gives me all of these reasons, and more. In the UK and the US, and in many other countries where Christianity is the majority religion, atheists are beginning to speak out against religion, to reverse the rising tide of fundamentalism which bases its morals on an ancient book, where God slaughters millions, slavery is condoned by Jesus, and non-believers are condemned to the eternal fire and damnation of Hell. I for one do not wish to live in a world where Christianity plays any visible part.

That is why I, and other atheists, vocalising their concerns in many different ways, speak out. Anti-racist movements have greatly reduced, though certainly not removed, racist beliefs in many countries. If atheists can remove some of the stigma associated with being openly atheist, our time will not have been wasted.

31

Hiding Opinions Behind the Bible

If you were God.

What would you do if you were the Christian God? Given many different choices, with alternative, easily definable outcomes, would you choose to act in exactly the same way as God?

If you were God, and you saw a woman being raped, would you save her? Would you lift her up and take her to a place of safety? Or would you leave her there, helpless and naked in the dirt, to be brutally used, and then discarded, or even murdered?

If you were God, and you heard the thoughts of a killer, would you calm those thoughts, convince him to step back and turn away, before he took out the knife, or pulled out the gun? If you were all-powerful you could simply make the weapon disappear, but if you wanted to remain unseen, then changing a potential murderer's thoughts would do the job. Nobody would know and you would save a life. Would you make that decision?

If a school caught fire and there were children inside being burned alive, would you save them? Or would you wait until they were dead, and tell them that because they were Hindu children, they would be condemned to burn forever, but this time in Hell, a Hell which you personally created for this purpose?

If a child born to Muslim parents, a child only 3 or 4 years old, was brought in front of you, would you consider it to be a vile, filthy, evil sinner? Would you take it by the hand and throw it into the fire and say, 'I made you, and I love you, but you are a sinner and disgusting to my sight. I never knew you.'? Is that what you would do if you were God?

If you were able, would you personally send for torture all homosexuals, sparing not a single one of them because they refused to accept that homosexuality is, in the eyes of a Christian, simply a choice, rather than a natural, some might say God-given, instinct?

Would you personally do these things if you had the powers of God and the choice was entirely yours?

The Bible teaches that God is all-knowing and all-powerful. He knows when an atrocity is about to be committed, and he can stop it if he chooses to do so. But of course he does not. Women are raped. People continue to be murdered. If God is truly there he could stop it, yet he chooses not to do so.

If that was you, could you ignore it? Could you possess total power over every part of the Universe, yet have no desire to help people in need?

Christianity teaches that the only way to God is through accepting Jesus Christ as your personal saviour. Muslims, Jews, Hindus, atheists, anyone but Christians, will be condemned to burn in Hell forever.

If you were God, would you be able to look a man, a woman or a child in the eye and say, simply because they followed the wrong religion, 'I judge you. I condemn you. I send you to Hell.'?

Accept the responsibility for your own opinions.

Many Christians are strongly anti-gay. They feel justified in the belief that homosexuality is a sin. It says so in the Bible, so there need be no debate.

Disliking, even hating someone's sexual preference is one thing, but would you, given the powers of God, throw each and every gay man and lesbian woman into a burning pit from which there was no escape?

If you were the Christian God, the God described in the Bible, that is exactly what you would do. But it's easy to devolve responsibility to this all-powerful being.

'God is up there and only he can judge,' say Christians. 'I am not here to judge, simply to give you my belief, my point of view,' a Christian might say, but then without an ounce of irony will add, '…which comes from the word of God'.

This arrogance is simply a sign that Christians transfer all responsibility and all opinions away from themselves and into the invisible hands of a mythical God. When someone says, 'Only God can judge,' what he really means is, 'I don't want to accept my part in the brutal justice system administered by my God. I don't even want to think about it. I refuse to say that this is my personally held opinion. I imply that it is, but if you want me to answer the accusation outright... sorry, take it up with God. I have no opinions of my own.'

Anyone who believes in God has to stand by the judgements of that God, and the teachings of the Bible. If you believe that God is right, then you *personally* approve of the torture of non-Christian children, and the burning of homosexuals. You personally would not intervene if you saw a murder or a rape about to happen. You personally believe that the correct punishment for all sins, however minor, is torture beyond measure, torment without end.

Because it's written doesn't mean it right.

When a Christian says that adultery is wrong 'because it says so in the Bible', but that he (the Christian) does not judge anyone, he is doing exactly that: judging the actions of individuals and groups of people in society, comparing them to God's standards, telling them they do not measure up, and explaining what they must do to be 'cured' of this wrongdoing.

'Those of you who want to ignore the Bible... well, it's your soul.' Another casual remark in the sly, seemingly innocent language of Christianity. What this actually means is, 'You must be punished for the slightest deviance from this book, and God will send you to suffer if you do not. And as a Christian, I approve of this.'

Yet Christians will not use these words. They will hide behind their belief that it is God's will, not theirs, and that they are unable to hold their own opinions because that would contradict the Bible, the supposedly inerrant, inspired word of God.

There is no grey area for the God of the Bible. There is simply right and wrong. If someone 'sins' a single time, perhaps something as small as a child taking a piece of candy from the kitchen without telling his mother, the punishment is an eternity spent in Hell. If you sin a million times, the punishment is the same. And of course if you rape, murder or steal you have the ultimate 'Get out of Jail Free' card. Simply be sorry, simply be Christian, and you will be spared.

Christianity teaches that nothing else on this Earth matters other than what is between you and God. If your heart is true to God, it doesn't matter what you've done. It is not about how many good deeds you do, the charity you give to others, the support and care you extend to your family, or to your fellow human beings. None of these things will be rewarded. Accepting Jesus is the only measure of worth in the Christian mindset.

The question we should be asking is: if good deeds mean absolutely nothing to God, what moral lessons can we learn from this? A Christian can point to a Muslim or a Jew and say with absolute certainty that that person's life is worthless. Nothing he does, nothing at all, other than conversion to Christianity, is of any consequence.

This is not a God who will reward you for anything you do, unless you serve, praise and offer your life up to him. This is not a moral viewpoint. It is certainly not a God promoting moral behaviour.

But then this is Christianity. What did you expect?

32

Cherry Picking, Prejudice and Hate

Choosing what God said.

Christian condemnation of homosexuality is one of the most obvious examples of modern-day religion using its 'holy' book to victimise gay men and women who are, after all, practising a legal, consensual activity. It accuses them of a mortal sin, for which they should be punished. To Christians, homosexuality is wrong, and their own personal opinions on the subject mean nothing. There is no debate: it says so in the Bible.

This is one example of cherry picking, selecting individual passages from the Bible which confirm a particular position: if the Bible is the word of God, then homosexuality is wrong. After all, there is little to dispute about the meaning of this passage:

> *If a man also lie with mankind, as he lieth with a woman, both of them have committed an abomination: they shall surely be put to death; their blood shall be upon them.*
>
> God (Leviticus 20:13)

Of course we don't put gay people to death these days, although there are a few Christians who preach that we should do exactly that. Some even want to stone adulterers. There are always a few nut-jobs who want every single rule in the Bible to stand today, in a modern society, thousands of years later. Thankfully they are in the minority.

However, if one part of the Bible is true and should be followed to the letter, surely there should be no exceptions. Surely these 'nut-jobs' have a point. If this book is, as Christians claim it to be, the inerrant word of God, we should indeed stone blasphemers (I'm in trouble), stone adulterers, sell thieves into slavery, marry anyone we entice into bed, and be killed just for working on the Sabbath. Mass executions of weekend-working Walmart employees are anticipated any time now.

The Bible doesn't have an 'errata' page at the end which says, 'by the way, these rules won't apply in 2000 years time so you can drop most of them'. Christian cherry picking involves not only insisting that some passages still hold true, but that passages from the Bible which are generally held to be *unacceptable* should be ignored.

The Bible was not written by God, it was written by men, in ancient times, and it certainly shows. You can be stoned for pretty much anything in the Bible – someone is stoned just for gathering sticks on the Sabbath (Numbers 15:32-36). And yes, I have genuinely, and in fact recently, seen a Christian defend that as justifiable punishment.

In general, society has dropped most of the Bible's barbaric punishments for minor crimes, and much of the behaviour is seen as unacceptable in our modern society. So why follow some parts and not others?

Whoever said slavery was acceptable?

Prejudice and self-interest seem to be a big part of the answer. Do whatever the Bible says, but only where it serves the interests of the people who believe in it. When the general public really start to object to it, well, pretend it never happened and that the Bible never mentions it.

When slavery was at its peak, the Bible was actively used to promote the idea that keeping slaves was an acceptable part of society. After all, if God didn't want us to have slaves, he wouldn't have mentioned slavery in the Bible would he? In fact Paul, an important figure in the New Testament, is probably slavery's number one fan. This is but one of the many times he mentions the keeping of slaves:

> *Let as many servants as are under the yoke count their own masters worthy of all honour, that the name of God and his doctrine be not blasphemed.*
> *God (1 Timothy 6:1)*

Some might argue that 'servant' is not the same as 'slave', but the language of the Bible is consistent:

> *And if a man smite his servant, or his maid, with a rod, and he die under his hand; he shall be surely punished. Notwithstanding, if he continue a day or two, he shall not be punished: for he is his money.*
> God (Exodus 21:20-21)

If this is a servant in the 'employee' sense of the word, you're hardly likely to beat him quite so severely, and the phrase 'for he is his money' clearly indicates that the 'servant' in this case is a possession. By any modern definition, this is a slave.

And while we're here: you can beat your servant with a rod so hard that you will only be punished if he doesn't live for a couple of days afterwards?

Nice lesson in morals – once again the Bible tells it like it is.

The woman's place.

Until relatively recently, the woman's place, by tradition, had been as the home maker, the housewife, and that is described in the Bible so that is the way things stood. Only the critical shortage of men to work in the factories during World War II started to put women into the workforce, and after its end attitudes to women at work were forced to change.

I once asked a work colleague why she always wore a hat to church. Her church, she told me, taught that women were secondary to men and that only men could uncover their heads in the presence of God. So although opinions change, perhaps the underlying current of strict Biblical 'truth' is still there in some places. And of course the Catholic Church is notable in that women are strictly forbidden from becoming priests. Indeed the Anglican Church was recently bitterly divided in its attempts to allow any such 'horror' as allowing a woman to lead a church service. Misogyny hasn't gone away, it seems.

Those old time prejudices.

Though some of the punishments may have softened or disappeared, many of the old prejudices remain. Of course the ultimate judge of what is right and what is wrong is, for Christians, their God, but that doesn't stop them picking out the juicy bits of the Bible which serve their purpose and feed their own prejudices.

The bottom line is that morals are not fixed, they are not set in stone, not even in stone tablets. Morals are based on society's acceptance of certain types of behaviour, which nowadays bear little resemblance to the archaic and brutal world which was the reality in Biblical times. We are living 2000 years after the supposed time of Jesus, and yet some of the same prejudices and hatreds still persist.

The only positive element of the story seems to be that society *has* come to accept that certain types of behaviour are wrong, *even if* it is written in the Bible. Adultery happens, single parent families happen, and we get on with life. No stoning, no imprisonment. No slavery.

We should persevere and put pressure on those who do not accept that times change, and make sure that something is done to change them. When the Bible's so-called 'morals' are no longer relevant in any way, there will finally be no more cherries for the Christians to pick.

Why God Won't Reveal Himself

Omnipotent. Omniscient. Omnipresent. And shy.

God's work has gone downhill since making the Universe in six days. It was a bit of a come-down from 'let there be light' to sending a plague of frogs to the Egyptians, and he hasn't recovered since. Parting the Red Sea should have been child's play, but right now about all God can manage is drawing his own face on frosty window panes.

He won't go out. He can't go out. He's in his safe place.

That's why nobody has seen him recently.

God has agoraphobia.

Rumours.

Or maybe he's just getting old and incontinent. A God who walks with man, but pisses himself in the street, is unlikely to maintain the respect of his followers. God doesn't do incontinence pants. That would be *so* demeaning to the Creator of the Universe. He tried to disguise the pee-pee as acid rain, but nobody was fooled. So he stays indoors, in Heaven, never more than 30 seconds away from a mop and bucket.

Things are bad for God these days.

Even worse, God could be forced to wear a colostomy bag. He won't appear on Earth because the gurgling sound as another turd forms itself in the little pouch is not something he is ready to share with two billion Christians. And those Muslims won't be very sympathetic you can bet.

Why God Won't Reveal Himself   153

Conceivably, in terms of miracles the Supreme Being may have shot his bolt and be taking a long time to recharge. Maybe dying on the cross took it out of him more than he expected. And the stitches haven't come out of his palms yet.

If God had a wife (and nobody is sure what the status of Mary is these days, since God put his bun in her oven), she'd have ditched him now for a God with a bit more go in him.

In Heaven Viagra has no power. God is impotent.

Vanity.

Some say that the collagen implants went horribly wrong and God now has the lips of a startled camel. The shame of a God who looks like he should have made man in the image of a sink plunger is all too much to bear.

You can laugh at bad sunburn, but would you want to reveal yourself to people who have been waiting 2000 years for a glimpse of your Holy face, only to find you are as red as a lobster and pealing badly? With nothing to do but wait for the date he's set for the Second Coming, can you blame God for catching some rays in one of the galaxies he made?

Maybe God is dead. Like Osama bin Laden, he was killed by a missile attack but nobody actually knew they'd done it, so the angels up there are keeping it out of the news. Because let's face it, that kind of publicity the religion does *not* need. Finding a replacement is taking some time in a Universe where there was only the one God.

He could have just died of old age. At the funeral nobody knew the protocol – who would hear the hymns, or answer the prayers? Satan did offer his services for the cremation, but burial in the family plot had always been the intention.

We don't actually know how old God is (or was). We're told he was 'always there', but as he only made the Earth 6000 years ago, maybe he is only in his 6020s. Making the Universe was his first job after leaving Universe University, and he's still embarrassed about that whole Flood incident and having to start all over again. And which one of the archangels made him bury all those non-working prototypes in the ground? Those humans only went and dug them up and used them to invent some fairytale which contradicts the Genesis story, didn't they? Oh the shame of it.

So God isn't coming out.

Alzheimer's makes God forgetful these days. 6020 is, after all, a ripe old age for anyone. The pictures in toast are about all he can manage, and Parkinson's Disease makes sure they aren't exactly works of art. When humans find the cure, God will come down to Earth, check himself in under a different name, and pop a few pills. Then he can make the comeback.

That is if God isn't still schizophrenic. He doesn't know who he is any more. Is he God the Father or God the Son? Maybe he's the Holy Spirit. The voices talk to him but he can never know. It's driving him insane.

Don't be shy.

Maybe God is just plain shy. Those Christians have so many expectations. It's hard to know if you can live up to that. The prayers and the devotion, they're all signs they want God to come back and make things just right.

What if he stutters, or trips and falls on the Pope? His first notable action might be to fart, two minutes into his Rapture speech.

Shyness could come from a number of equally disturbing directions. God could be having a bad hair day. Opening the back gate of Heaven when Satan's next door having a barbecue is a bad idea – the hot wind blows through, and messes up your mullet big time. Yes, God has a mullet. Heavenly at the front, devilish round the back.

Whoops, that huge spot on the nose is a no-no for public appearances. And no clean underpants – what if someone saw the skidmarks as he floated overhead? And God does *not* go commando.

But God, with all those adoring fans ready to praise you, why not take a chance? Make the first move. Come out of the closet.

At least make a video and post it on YouTube, or start a MySpace account – everyone does it these days. So someone already took the God domain name, so what? Omnipotence counts for a lot at the domain registry. Take back *god.com* and show what an Intelligent Web Designer can do!

The Fame Game.

Maybe the problem is that fame isn't all fun and games. Let's face it, God will be totally mobbed by his adoring fans, maybe people pulling at his beard, ripping his clothes, just to get a piece of him. Shit, even Pastor Ted would throw his lil' panties onto the stage if God Himself did a one-nighter in San Francisco.

Admittedly God's wardrobe has gone out of fashion. He really doesn't want to be a laughing stock, but the platform shoes and the glam rock eye shadow, which he waited for thousands of years to come into vogue, well, they didn't last very long. God doesn't want to give up the big hair, the lipstick, the glitter shirts. He's waiting for them to come back into fashion.

Kiss were never the same without the make-up.

Most of all, God may be fed up that Christians are doing a really shit job of spreading the message of peace and love, by actually preaching division and intolerance. What was the reason for the hundreds of different sects of Christianity again? God was just about to drop in during the 16th century to thank the Catholics for doing a great job, albeit with a couple of hints on toning the Inquisition down a little, and then what happens? Bang, Martin Luther goes and messes up the whole system, splitting the Church up into little pieces.

God won't come down again until everyone gets back to that old-style Roman Catholicism. And as for those Evangelical pricks, God has some real fun lined up for them in the after-life. Think chestnuts roasting on an open fire. Christmas will never be the same for those guys.

God is waiting. He's watching. He's planning it all down to the last detail. He's all seeing, all knowing, all powerful.

But God isn't happy. He's just going to sit in Heaven and look down at his feet, where all the little people are fighting below, and be sad.

God cries wretched tears of misery for atheists everywhere.

God is empty.

God is emo.

And he won't come out of his room.

God Almighty's Genesis Diary – Day 5

Day 5 – Friday

7:00 am

Animal day. Oh joy. So now I get to build millions of scuttly little insects while at the same time the bigger creatures will probably stomp around and crush everything. Great.

You'll notice I'm up bright and early. This will not be a repeat of the vegetation fiasco. Why not? Because, dear diary, I have a secret weapon, and, oh well, nobody is actually going to read this, so…

Random chance.

That's right. God said 'let there be random chance'. Sometimes you wake up with a stiffy, sometimes you wake up with an idea, and this idea is all mine. And oh, momma, it is *good*.

I sniff a promotion, I smell 'worker of the month'. Time for a shower and a change of socks, now I come to think of it.

There'd better be some kind of salary increase in this. While everyone else farts around with individual creatures, I just build what I call 'kinds' and everything else is on auto-pilot – they just sort of change into lots of other interesting stuff. And the best thing is, nobody will *ever* work this out. They'll all just think I made everything by hand, one by one.

Cos I really have the time for that don't I?!

I'm thinking of patenting the process. This could evolve into something really big for me if I can get it licensed to other Creators. I just need to evolve a name for it, but the excitement has gone to my head and I can't think. Oh well, I'll let the ideas evolve a little more and maybe something will pop into my mind.

7:15 am

I've got it. Randochaosity. It's a winner!

7:25 am
I'd better make a start. I still have to sort out the 'kinds' before I start the 'randochaosity' process churning out the rest of the species.

10:30 am
Look at that, three short hours and we're all ready to go. I have lizards, fish and birds. So that's land, sea and air completely covered. Five kinds each, just for a bit of variety, and they're primed for inter-breeding, so plenty of scope for all kinds of different species. They're all lined up and ready to go, I just need to say the Word.

10:35 am
Okay, I wrote it down somewhere, where is it?

10:45 am
Go!

12:30 pm
Things are cooking nicely. The fish kinds seem to be a bit of a weak link because they all look pretty similar, but I've mixed up some extra gunk in there and managed to get some ugly looking squid and a couple of enormous sharks. Nasty.

The land animals are pretty good, no complaints there. I started with the plant eaters and sent them all off to chew on some of the cheaper bushes up north, nothing that I couldn't replace. I think I can just leave them to it. Nice.

Birds. Hmm. As I've only got one day, I really need them to learn to fly as soon as possible, but they're all just flapping around, squawking a lot and mating like there was no tomorrow. And there won't be if they don't start mingling and popping out some other species. I'd better get down there and move this on myself.

2:25 pm
Is it me or am I destined to get shit on from a great height every single day of my damned life? Inter-breeding locks are off, yes? So some idiot land animal only goes and falls into the sea, humps a shark and gives me sea creatures that breathe air. What the…? You cannot swim and breathe air at the same time! Whales, dolphins, what next? Birds that swim?

2:50 pm

Very funny. Oh, I'm splitting my sides over this one. Penguins. Not only can they swim, they can't even fly. Not even a little bit. Shit, the fuckers have trouble even walking.

You want worse? Some of the lizards can fly better than the frigging birds! Even some of the fish have got wings now!

I've had to switch off the whole inter-breeding process, which means randochaosity needs some serious fine tuning.

3:15 pm

Okay. Land animals can now only mate with other land animals. Same goes for air-with-air, and the swimmers bone only other water creatures. I'm going to have to keep the hybrids though, they've gone forth and multiplied and it will be impossible to catch them all in time.

4:10 pm

Don't ask.

4:15 pm

Really. Do not ask.

4:20 pm

Remember I put the plant eaters in the 'bushes'? Well from a distance it looked like they were doing well, so I threw in a dash of carnivore, because we all like a good fight, and I'm as bloodthirsty as the next Supreme Being. Meat eaters were popping out all over the place. Job's a good un.

That was maybe 1:00 pm, and because of the inter-breeding cock-ups elsewhere I was happy to let them get on with it and just concentrate on the bigger picture.

Except the 'bushes' were actually 400-foot high rain forests, and that's right, the randochaosity scaled my animals up to fit their surroundings in double-quick time.

This is terrible. All my lizards are so big they are going to strip the planet bare in no time. The carnivores are ripping each other to bits, and all the herbivores are so hungry they're treating my lush greenery like an all-you-can-eat restaurant.

Terrible lizards at the end of what should have been a wonderful day. And today I am right out of time, completely done for.

4:45 pm

Drastic situation, drastic measures. They're going to have to go. I've cooked up some toxins, put them into fifty globes, and they are orbiting the planet right now. I just need to say the word and down they come – the big lizards will be history.

There's one problem. Everything has to be audited. Everything. If I say 'let the terrible lizards die', the Big Boss is going to know about it. And randochaosity isn't going to look like such a great invention any more. I need someone else for this. Someone to take the heat.

6:15 pm

This is off the record, but I have just the man. He's a contact from the old days, back when the Universe was still a pretty dark place, but he knows some people in the business, who'll do it for cash up front, no questions asked. I'm meeting him in a bar called 'Praises', in the east end of town, later tonight. Right now I just need to call in a few favours, and get together enough gold, frankincense and, what's this? Myrrh? WTF? Well if they want it, I'll get it. I'm past caring.

9:30 pm

Damn. If I'd known it was the three King Brothers I'd never have got into this. This is some deep and dirty shit I'm wading in, up to my neck. My contact took the bag, and says it's as good as done. And when the Kings get in on the act, you know they mean business.

11:15 pm

It's done. The big lizards are all dead. The Kings even tidied up the corpses, buried them underground, way down deep in the rocks, somewhere nobody will ever find them. Credit where it's due, those guys do a good job. But I feel a little tarnished by this. I never felt so, well... all I can call it is sinful.

Tomorrow I still have to make all the land animals again, and meanwhile I will have to erase all my records. At least the birds and the fish worked out okay.

What a day. What a God awful day.

35

Biggest Bullshit Bible Story – Part 1

Two by two.

There is a story in the Bible which is so important to Fundamentalist Christians that even some of the miracles of Jesus himself might have to take second place when compared to it. It is so essential to Christian 'scientists' that they base their entire refutation of modern science on this legend. There is simply no more vital story in the Christian war against science than this.

And yet within that bumper book of fantastical tales, the Bible, it is the biggest bullshit story of all. This is the story of the Great Flood and of Noah's Ark[1], on which rest the shaky foundations of Fundamentalist Christian 'science'. Fundies believe the Bible to be the inerrant word of God, therefore science, evidence and common sense are all swept aside and replaced by unshakeable, unquestioning faith in this story.

It's so laughable it isn't even funny.

The Flood is important because it is a Biblical story which has apparently, *allegedly*, left significant physical evidence. It provides the 'proof' that Christians so desperately need to justify their belief in the assertion that God is responsible for life on Earth, and that the Universe is only 6,000 years old.

The basic premise of the myth is that God wants to destroy all life on Earth, tells Noah he will save him, his family and two of every creature, and that he must build an Ark, load up the animals and look out for bad weather.

---

[1] The bullshit runs into volumes, so I recommend further reading on this subject: http://www.talkorigins.org/faqs/faq-noahs-ark.html

Building the Ark.

The longest wooden ships built in modern times were much less than 400 feet long and leaked so badly that water needed to be pumped out of them constantly. Unstable, and largely unseaworthy, these vessels were only suitable for short hauls in fine weather. They were at the limit of what was possible in wooden ship construction and suffered from severe structural problems.

The Bible says that the Ark was 450 feet long, give or take a cubit or two. Structurally it is unlikely that the Ark would be any more seaworthy, and certainly no less prone to leaking, so would also have had to be continuously pumped out. Bear in mind there are only eight people on the boat. This is only the first of the many tasks they will have to perform.

Gathering the animals.

Problem: the world is a big place. Emus from Australia, tigers from India, polar bears from the Arctic. This is 2500 BC – no jet travel, no motor transport. Wagons and horses are the best they have.

Even if you send out expeditions all over the planet, some animals have only a short life span. You might spend years searching for a particular type of mouse, or lizard, or insect, only to have it die before you get back. Oops.

Special climate-controlled conditions would be needed to bring back the more sensitive species, just like the containers used by modern zoos. Which of course did not exist in 2500 BC.

This assumes that humans go and fetch the animals. But the Bible says *they* came to Noah, a different and much bigger problem.

Some animals don't travel well overland. Sloths aren't exactly champion sprinters, to take a good example. Koalas – slow too, but they also have a special diet, so imagine them packing a big sack full of eucalyptus leaves to take with them on the journey. The several thousand *mile* journey from Australia to the Middle East.

Changes in climate would kill many species. They would overheat, or, crossing a mountain range, they might freeze to death. Swimming across vast oceans is impossible. Especially if you're an ostrich or a kangaroo.

And again, each animal would lack continuous access to their primary food sources, necessary for survival.

Imagine all these animals wandering thousands of miles across the world, two of each kind, looking around as they pass the other predators who won't be joining them on the Ark, thinking 'please don't eat me' as they approach them. Remember, *thousands* of miles.

Could all the animals have lived locally? That would solve the travel problem. Yet you'd need to find a place suitable for penguins and alligators, giraffes and lizards, and everything in-between. The Middle East is not it.

4500 years ago, around 2500 BC, none of this is possible or plausible.

Fitting them all on board.

There are too many species to fit on board the Ark. So the explanation given today is that Noah didn't take every species, he instead took every *kind* of animal. Instead of tigers, lions, cheetahs and leopards, there was just one kind of cat.

This begs the question: when the animals came off the Ark, they needed to mutate quickly into all the other species. *Very* quickly in fact. Even 4500 years wasn't enough, because many species are mentioned in ancient recorded history, so would have to have appeared by then.

Which of the many different cats would be taken? The tigers might not produce non-stripey offspring very effectively. If Noah saved the cheetahs, could he be sure that they would produce the shaggy mane of a lion, or the stumpy tail of a bobcat? Certainly humans have helped to create many breeds of dogs and cats, but the Bible makes no mention of the eight people on the Ark setting up selective breeding programmes for the main 'types' on board, including rescued felines.

Of course those who believe the story don't believe in evolution. And yet in maybe one or two thousand years, all big cats must have evolved from a single common ancestor. Sounds like evolution on steroids!

Evolution actually needs huge amounts of time to work, but the same people who don't believe that fact do believe that evolution can work on a large scale in a short amount of time. Do they actually *know* what they believe?

This is not possible. And the alternative, that evolution doesn't happen, is worse: Noah would have to take two of *every* species, including ones which later became extinct. Thousands and thousands and thousands of species of animals, some of which (many insects for example) don't even breed in pairs. And some, including thousands of different species of termite, might find the Ark's wooden hull a very tasty proposition indeed.

Did someone mention food? Bear in mind that the Flood waters didn't subside for about a year, so Noah had to take enough food on board to feed two of every animal in the world for a year. That's a lot of food.

Especially if you're an elephant, eating 300-600 pounds of food every day (50-100 tons each, over the year). Or the meat-eating lions, who like the look of the two tasty antelopes who live just down the corridor.

Dinosaurs.

Yes indeed, if you believe the Bible 'science', dinosaurs had to have been on the Ark. The dinosaur fossils we have were created by the Flood (see later), so dinosaurs must have been saved, two by two.

Dinosaurs can be big. Some are *really* big. Maybe Noah found baby dinos? No, the Bible says two of every kind, a male and his mate, so they must have been adults, if the Bible is correct of course. A boat-load of full-size dinosaurs. Imagine that.

I know I can't.

Caring for the animals.

How did Noah and only seven other people care for all these animals for a whole year? I've touched on special diets, needed by koalas, pandas, even silkworms, which eat only mulberry leaves, but in truth *all* animals have their own particular dietary requirements. Some even need fresh, live prey. Tricky, when there are only two of each animal on board.

No tin cans, no refrigeration. Even until a couple of hundred years ago, food spoiling and infestation by insects or rats was a problem, and that was just the food needed by the crew. We're talking about thousands of species, thousands of different food types, all needing food preservation for a whole year.

Imagine thousands of animals, of all sizes, and the waste they will create, which all has to be dealt with. Add to that methane from the back end and carbon dioxide from the front end. Suddenly the 18-inch gap at the top of the Ark, which Bible scholars believe was the only ventilation, is looking pretty small.

I emphasise this again: eight people, eight humans, are the only ones on the Ark to take care of every species of animal in the world. Imagine the biggest zoo you've ever visited. Now imagine you and seven others looking after every single animal in that zoo and carrying all the shit from all the rooms on all the decks, and shoving it over the side of the Ark. You've got a lot of work to do, because you've also got to feed the animals and exercise them too – if the animals don't get exercise, their muscles are going to start wasting away.

Can eight people look after tens of thousands of animals, on a leaky boat, in choppy seas? What do you think?

Who can argue with the Bible? It's the word of God, right? Fundamentalist Christians believe this bullshit *to the letter*, and their Creation 'science' is built around it.

But the story gets worse. Much worse.

Here comes the rain...

Biggest Bullshit Bible Story – Part 2

Miracles are easy. Science takes evidence.

The Noah's Ark story is of vital importance to Fundamentalist Christians because it underpins their entire rejection of evolution, the age of the Universe, the fossil record, and the abundance of evidence which supports all of these things. In particular, its incredible claims launch a full-scale attack on the science of geology, the most basic principles of which are completely thrown out of the window.

With an unlikely number of animals on board an equally improbable wooden vessel, we can now examine the events of the Flood itself.

The first things to ask are: where did the flood waters come from, and where did they go? Christians have at various times put forward some ever more ludicrous suggestions, trying to use science to prove it all happened. In my opinion you can solve all of these problems just by saying 'God did a miracle'. Easy! But no, Christians have to make it really difficult for themselves and use science instead.

In simple terms, the Christian position seems to be that the rain came from a vapour canopy surrounding the Earth; from a huge underground store of water; or both.

Vapour Canopy.

The rain water was suspended in a kind of vapour canopy over the Earth, which fell as rain and flooded the entire planet.

Firstly, how did the water stay up there? We're talking about water falling everywhere on Earth, all at once, to a depth of hundreds, possibly thousands of feet, and that's just when it's a mass of sea water. As vapour any 'canopy' would have to be much deeper than that because it would have to float in the atmosphere as tiny droplets.

The canopy's thickness would hugely increase atmospheric pressure. When you dive underwater to any depth, pressure increases, and the greater the pressure the greater the danger to your body. It doesn't matter if the water's above you in the sea (diving), or if it's above you in the sky (vapour canopy), the extra pressure is going to be enormous.

Consider how dark it gets on a really cloudy day before a storm. Now imagine that the entire world had always lived under a cloud canopy, but even darker than that. Solid cloud, since the world began. Before the Flood, plants wouldn't grow, simply because most of them need sunlight. A canopy that thick would block out a huge amount of light, which would significantly lower the temperature of the Earth. It would be like a nuclear winter. You wouldn't even be able to see the open sky, or the sun.

The idea is madness. The Flood has to cover everything, including the mountains, so is it credible that that much water could stay up in the sky without having any effect on the world below it?

Hydroplate.

The hydroplate describes another suggestion by Creation 'science' that a layer of water, miles below the surface, was released when the Earth's crust broke open, and contributed to the Flood.

Bear in mind that the further down you go, the smaller the diameter, so to get 100 feet of water at the surface, you might need 150 feet of water further down, because it's wrapped around a smaller core. And we're looking for enough water to cover all the mountains of the Earth. Hmm. Where was all this water kept again?

Rock isn't naturally buoyant, and although you can have underground caverns, that's because the open spaces are supported by surrounding rocks. We're talking about thousands of feet of water around the whole of the Earth, which is what you'd need if you had to flood the entire surface. So with the Earth's crust pressing down, any water would have been forced up and out long before any Flood.

And what about the temperature? Even a mile down, the Earth is extremely hot, so the water at that depth would be superheated and blast upwards as hot steam. Instead of the Great Flood we would have had the Great Steam Cleaning, and Noah would have invented the first laundry service.

There is *no* geological evidence for this at all. If such colossal quantities of water had escaped from below the Earth there would have been massive damage, and obvious evidence of collapsing in order to fill the gaps, enormous signs of activity left in the geology of the Earth. But there is nothing like that anywhere on the planet.

Once again, this is just a mad Christian idea, designed by someone who is trying to fit science into a place where it just doesn't want to go.

After the Flood, where did the water go?

Fundamentalist Christians believe that the water didn't just disappear, but that it's still here, and this is what fills our oceans. The reason we're not still covered with water is that before the Flood the Earth was much flatter, and so easier to cover. Afterwards, through some 'cataclysmic events' (which God forgot to mention in the Bible), the mountains were pushed up and the ocean floors were lowered, and so the Flood water just sank into the ocean basins.

All this happened in the space of a year. The entire surface of the Earth moved underneath the sea, forming the mountains and the ocean beds. What a wonderful thing Christian scientists have shown us!

How is this all possible unless you use miracles?

Perhaps a quarter of the Earth's crust would have to be moved in the space of a year in order to create the mountains and the deep ocean basins. Remember how big the waves are when a single earthquake under the sea causes a tsunami. The waves are hundreds of feet high even with a fairly localised earthquake.

But we're talking about movements of the Earth's crust that are going to produce mountains as high as Everest – five *miles* high. Imagine how big a movement it would take to create that, if it all happened within one year.

If the Earth rose up so quickly, the water would drain away in huge torrents around the various continents of the world. But there is no physical evidence that this ever happened. None.

Yet while all this chaos is going on, while mountains are forming and oceans floors are sinking, among all the tsunamis covering the entire world, there's a little boat happily bobbing around on the surface, filled with animals, with Noah and his family shovelling the shit of tens of thousands of sea-sick creatures over the side.

Aaarrrr! 'Tis stormy seas!

Implications of a Flood.

One Flood, 4500 years ago, means that the geological timescales necessary for gradual erosion of the landscape did not happen. So why are some of the Earth's mountain ranges eroded much more than others? In general, newly formed mountains (eg the Sierra Nevada) have a jagged appearance, and are much higher, while 'old' mountains (eg the Appalachians) are generally much flatter, and rounder, as you would expect from being eroded for many millions of years longer. After the Flood, all erosion would have been the same, therefore all mountain ranges would look similar. This is not the case.

Ice cores can be dated back 40,000 years or more because ice is deposited annually on the polar ice caps. Changes in salt levels would be the least you would expect to find after global flooding. There is no such evidence of a global flood.

Such a flood would not have left the ice caps in place. Considering the depth of water needed to cover the Earth, the polar ice would simply have floated away and broken apart. And 4500 years is not nearly enough time for the ice to reform to such a depth.

Evidence from the ocean floors is also missing. Where is the mix-up of rocks of all sizes, of dead animals, of human tools, the chaotic jumble of everything on land which was swept away by the Flood? Instead, we find layer upon layer of rocks and sediment which could only have been deposited in a gradual, orderly way.

None of the evidence we have points towards a cataclysmic event on a global scale. Moreover, the 'science' of the 'vapour canopy' and the 'hydroplate' just makes no sense. It could never happen. It would literally take a miracle.

Just say God did it.

The thing that Christians seem to forget is that the more they try to twist the scientific evidence to fit their crazy story, the more stupid that story looks. 'Vapour canopy' and 'hydroplate' all sound wonderfully, but superficially, scientific, but they just don't hold up even to the simplest scientific examination.

What baffles me is why Christians even bother trying to use science. If they already think that God created the Earth in six days, well why didn't he also create a boat, conjure all the animals onto it, make the water appear, and a year later make it disappear again, then plant all the fossils underground, in order, so that the fossil record looks exactly like the scientists say it would look if the Earth was billions of years old?

If you just say 'God did it', it's so much easier!

Biggest Bullshit Bible Story – Part 3

Back to school.

You might think that parts 1 and 2 of this demolition of the Biblical Flood story pretty much destroy the Christian Fundamentalist position. But so far I've only touched very briefly on the so-called 'scientific' evidence which Christians use to explain the Flood. To understand this more fully we need to cover a little basic science, to compare *real* science with Christian 'science'.

You will probably have seen exposed sections of mountains, cliff faces or valleys, where it's possible to see different layers of rock, called strata. Most of the rocks that are visible are *sedimentary* rocks, which means they were formed by the deposition of sediment. See, science is easy!

Sediment comes from rivers, lakes, ocean floors, or flooding, anywhere that water can carry particles of silt, or where organisms die and sink to the bottom. Over time as the layers build up, they are compacted down by the weight of all the material above them. Remember that rocks go miles down into the Earth, so the pressure is immense.

It's easy to see why sedimentary rocks contain fossilised animals. For example, an animal might die in a swamp, then over time the swamp would silt up, and over millions of years under the right conditions the layers would be compacted and turned into rock.

There are other kinds of rocks: igneous rocks, formed when magma cools and solidifies, either on the surface or underground; and metamorphic rocks, where existing rock comes under different temperature or pressure conditions and changes into a different kind of rock.

However, sedimentary rocks are found on 75% of the world's surface, and so are the most important. These are the rocks where we usually find fossils, and before radiometric dating methods they were the only way we could date fossils – the further down the strata we find a fossil, the older it is, and the further up the strata, the more recently it died.

If you found a human fossil below a dinosaur fossil there would be problems, but so far that hasn't happened, and the fossil record is consistent with the idea that animals have died over a long period of time, and have been buried under layer upon layer of sediment, which eventually turned into rock under the immense pressure from the material above it.

What happened when radiometric dating came in was that we no longer had to rely on simply examining the rock layers to assert that the fossils at the top were more recent than the ones lower down. Radiometric dating lets us date the rocks, and so date the fossils.

It's important to remember that *even if* there was no radiometric dating we could still date the rocks and the fossils. Christian scientists tend to say that radiometric dating is garbage, but science doesn't need it to prove its case. It's just nice to have it, to make an already strong case even stronger, because the dates from the rocks do match up exactly how we'd expect them to match up if the rocks lower down were old, and the ones further up were younger.

That is a basic idea of what science uses to look at how the Earth was put together, how we date things, and why there are layers of rock, and fossils embedded in those rocks. Of course a more detailed study of geology will give you a better understanding of the processes involved, so I urge you to read further on the subject.

The importance of being in denial.

How does Fundamentalist Christianity try to explain the geological evidence? Well, it seems that the Earth was made in 6 days, about 6000 years ago, then approximately 4500 years ago the planet was flooded and every living thing on it was killed, except the people and animals in the Ark. Everything that we find in geology today was laid down in a single year, during the Flood.

That's what they believe. All the rocks, all the fossils, and also all the continents, oceans, mountains, everything that we consider under the heading of 'geology', were all formed in *one year*.

This is why this story is so important to Christian science. If all the animals were killed at once, evolution was unnecessary, because the animals later found as fossils would have been alive together, and so they died together. If the Earth is only 6000 years old there was no time for evolution to happen – evolution takes millions of years to produce so many different species of animal.

Remember that a single rock stratum, just one type of rock, can be hundreds or thousands of feet thick. There are layers on layers of these rocks, one on top of the other. But the Fundamentalist Christians believe that these thousands of feet of rocks were all laid down in one year, in one Flood.

What about the fossils? Obviously they were laid down at the same time as the sedimentary rocks, which fits in with the story because the animals were all swept away and killed in the Flood. Why, though, do we find the simpler fossils way, way down in the lower layers, and why do the more complex fossils only start to appear further and further up?

Science explains this very easily. The simple life forms are at the bottom because simple life forms evolved first, died first, and were covered in sediment first. More complex life forms, right up to the dinosaurs and beyond, evolved later, died later, and were covered in sediment later. So you'd expect them to be higher up in the fossil record, which is also what we find.

So how do Christians explain this?

There are two explanations, and I hope you're ready for this, because your levels of incredulity will be stretched to breaking point.

Run!

The first, and the funniest, is that when the Flood waters came down, the more complex and agile animals were able to run faster, so they could get out of the way by climbing up the mountains. All the snails and slugs are at the bottom of the fossil record because they weren't able to escape. Just above them are the lizards and amphibians, who could run, but not quite fast enough, and above that are the birds and mammals, who were a lot better runners and fliers. Humans were so clever that they climbed the mountains right to the top, and were killed by the Flood last of all.

Seriously, that's the story some Christians are taught to believe. I kid you not. Are you still wondering why 'Christian science' is an oxymoron?

Float!

The other explanation is a little more detailed, but it's still utterly ridiculous. The fossils were apparently deposited according to what is called the 'hydrodynamic properties' of the dead animals. This is referred to by Creationists as 'hydrologic sorting'.

In essence this means that simple animals, like slugs and snails and so on, sank to the bottom very quickly. As before, lizards and amphibians and dinosaurs floated in the water a while longer before they sank too. And then mammals and birds and humans all managed to float even longer before they too sank below the flood waters and became fossils.

Okay, I can probably stop right now because common sense is telling you that this is all complete bullshit. What Fundamentalist Christians are saying is this: the faster you run, or the better you float, the higher up you'll be in the fossil record.

That is all they have. And on purely that basis they reject evolution. They believe that the fossils in thousands of feet of rock strata have been sorted into order simply because some animals float or run better than others. This is what they are using to make themselves believe that evolution has no scientific basis.

The real flood starts here.

Here then is the evidence, as if you needed any more, that what the Christian 'scientists' say is complete and utter bullshit. Here's the science. Here is where we utterly destroy this stupid Flood story, so what follows is a flood of my own: a flood of common sense, easily verifiable facts, which will bury Noah's Ark as if it never existed. Which of course it never did.

Let's start with running to high ground. Why didn't at least one dinosaur make it to the high ground with the elephants? Some dinosaurs are very similar to present-day animals. So why aren't their fossils found together?

This applies to the sinking theory as well. Why would a dinosaur the shape and size of a pig be found, but no modern pigs found at the same level?

If the birds made it to the high ground, why didn't Pteranodons or other flying dinosaurs?

If all the animals were sorted according to how fast they sank, why are some molluscs such as snails and shellfish found all the way up the fossil record? They should have all descended to the same level, surely?

Let's look at coral reefs. A coral reef is a band of living organisms which grow underwater and form a solid mass of life. Reefs build up in layers, so when old organisms die, new ones grow on top. These aren't just single animals dying and forming layers. It takes time to build up a coral reef, and the one-year Flood just isn't time enough.

In fact some coral reefs are hundreds of feet thick and several miles long. And *under* those coral reefs are fossils. I'm not talking about the reefs that we have now. These are coral reefs which are themselves fossils, but which have other fossils below them. For that to happen, the reef would have had to break off in a big chunk, wait for animals to sink beneath it, then plant itself back down on top. Does that sound sensible?

Back to sinking organisms again. The lower fossil layers contain mainly small organisms. But a little something called fluid mechanics says that they would not sink to the bottom quickly at all. Some are quite buoyant and would sink slowly, and would end up in the upper layers.

If it's all down to how quickly things sink, how come there are no human tools found in the lower layers? Presumably the wood for the Ark was cut down with axes, so they had the technology to make metal tools. Where are the axe heads mixed with the dinosaur bones? We do find axe heads and early tools, but not embedded thousands of feet down within sedimentary rocks.

Fossil footprints are a favourite of mine. These are found near the habitats of extinct creatures, as you would expect. But you only find footprints where you find the creatures who made them. So somehow, the footprints of a dinosaur managed to sink under the flood waters at the same rate as the animal itself.

I have yet to mention fossil plants. Trees and bushes don't tend to run for shelter. How are *they* sorted in order from the least complex to the most advanced?

There are more things that we find in the rock strata that shouldn't be there if the Flood account is true. Deep down in the geological record you find evidence of river channels. How did rivers make channels when the whole of the Earth was under water? And how do we find evidence of trees growing in the middle of the fossil record, when surely the trees should have been ripped up and/or buried, all in the same layer?

What about animal burrows that are all found deep down in the rock layers? If the animals were underwater and presumably dead, it's unlikely they were digging around making shelters for themselves.

Cave systems. We know that cave systems are hollowed out of solid rocks by water action, over many, many years. Sometimes they fill up again with silt. But how would the caves form *and* fill up at the same time if everything was being deposited under water all at once? Filled-in caves are found in different rock strata, so it's just not possible that this could be caused by one big Flood.

Kiss my rebuttal.

Here's some more science for you. Angular unconformities are found when layers of rock are deformed somehow, maybe tilted or pushed upwards from below by natural processes (for an illustration, take this book and flex it into a curve, imagining the pages are rock strata). Then the top is worn down by erosion, leaving a flattened surface. Finally, more sediment is laid on top, forming more rock strata.

This kind of thing couldn't happen in a single event. You need layers of rock, which are then bent out of shape, worn down, and covered over again. Not possible in the Flood.

The Flood story also doesn't explain how deep marine limestone, which is made up of the tiny fossils of creatures which lived on the ocean floor, managed to become part of the summit of Mount Everest, *five miles* up. With real science the explanation is that mountains are formed when two tectonic plates collide and push each other up to form mountains, but Christian science has no answer for this at all, unless you believe that the Himalayas were built in one year.

Let's have a look at the detailed layering of the sedimentary rocks. One formation in New Jersey is six kilometres thick. If we give hundreds of days (one year) for this to settle, we still have 15 metres of sediment settling *per day*.

Yet despite this speedy deposition, there are big changes in the chemical properties of the rocks. If the Flood was so violent, how do we explain a thin layer of *high* carbonate sediment, which would have had only 30 minutes to settle, followed by 30 minutes of *low* carbonate sediment? Perhaps a local incident? Not so. These strata cover an area of 10,000 square kilometres. The most cataclysmic event in the history of the Earth apparently still managed to lay down vast, but relatively thin, sheets of sediment, with the lightest of touches.

This is the scale of the problem, but Christian scientists think they can describe the whole process with one huge Flood in an impossibly small time scale.

What about forests? The fossil record includes not just animals, but fossil forests as well. In some areas we find several forests stacked on top of one another, with the trees still upright. One example is 2750 metres thick, (over 1.5 miles). Some of these forests have hundreds of feet of rock strata between them, and some show evidence of forest fires. Fires? In a flood? How did that happen?

And these are not just simple logs falling vertically through the water, we are talking about whole forests with the roots still intact.

How did limestone get there? Limestone is made up of billions of microscopic sea animals. Some limestone beds are thousands of metres thick. That means that all the animals in the limestone had to have been alive during the Flood. Imagine a mile of rock, then imagine that the creatures are all alive and swimming around, obviously taking up a lot more room when they are alive.

One big question this leads to is: where were all the fossilised animals when they were alive? Christian scientists say that in some places there are so many fossils that it just proves they were all killed at once. But if they were all alive at once, there would actually be no room on the planet for everything to move around.

In one area, a thousand-kilometre stretch of the Arctic coast, there are estimated to be about 500,000 *tons* of tusks. Even assuming that the entire population was preserved, Russia would have had wall-to-wall mammoths before the Flood.

More science: the coal reserves that we find under the Earth are made up from compressed organic materials such as forests. Even if a single continuous forest covered the entire planet, there would still not be enough to account for the coal reserves and other organic sediments found beneath the Earth. So where did all the organic deposits come from? It's impossible that they were all laid down in a single Flood.

This is the big one.

This chapter has still only scratched the surface of the available scientific evidence, but you can easily see that Fundamentalist Christians who believe in the Biblical Flood really don't have a prayer when it comes to explaining the *real* evidence that *real* scientists can produce.

Maybe that's the problem. The people who are spreading the Christian 'science' must know about these facts, but they just don't tell anybody about them. And the average person, whatever their religion, isn't going to go investigating and reading through geology textbooks and scientific papers.

They believe what they are told, and they have no opinion about the real evidence, because they don't even know about it.

Remember that Christian 'science' is trying to tell you that everything you see around you, all the mountains, all the seas, all the many layers of rock, all the fossils, were all laid down in *one year*, approximately 4500 years ago.

You now have some idea of how immense the problem is. Fundamentalist Christian science is based on *this* story. They use their so-called evidence as the basis for their rejection of evolution, the geological record, and the age of the Earth. They truly believe that the Noah's Ark story is genuine, and they don't care what they have to do to convince you. They will take any scientific facts you care to mention and just throw them away.

God's salty salvation.

I haven't even gone into events *after* the Flood. How did the animals get to all the different continents, supposedly formed during the Flood? Where did all the trees and plants start growing? The Earth would presumably have no soil after it was washed away and covered over with sediment. What there was would be full of salt, sludge and debris which would kill most plant life.

Plant life? What plant life? Unless Noah took every species of plant onto the Ark too, they would all be dead, extinct, buried by the sediment, the miles and miles of sediment containing all the future fossils... remember? So where exactly did Noah's dove find an olive leaf?

The weight of evidence should completely and utterly destroy the Noah's Ark story, and its flimsy basis for rejection of the fossil record. And if anyone can still say they believe in the Biblical Flood after what you've just read, they need some serious medical attention!

Flood Fossil Fantasies

A giant of a problem.

I'm going to give you a few assumptions, and remember that these are Christian beliefs not mine, so no quoting me out of context please:

1. The Bible is 100% true and accurate because it is the word of God, who is perfect.

2. The Great Flood brought down by God to cleanse the Earth killed everybody except the people and animals in the Ark. So all the fossils that we find are evidence of animals killed by the Flood, and not evidence of evolution.

3. Evolution is false because there are gaps in the fossil record. Some species that evolutionists expect to be there simply aren't found as fossils.

So if the Bible is true, if the Flood really happened and it created all the fossils, and missing fossils prove evolution to be false...

Where are all the fossils of giants?

The Bible mentions giants several times, such as in Genesis 6:4, *'There were giants in the earth in those days; and also after that, when the sons of God came in unto the daughters of men.'*

Well actually this is the only mention of giants *before* the Flood, which is strange because they are mentioned quite often *after* the Earth has been re-populated – shouldn't the Flood have killed all these giants? We'll ignore this little mistake (oops, the Bible isn't perfect and we're only as far as Genesis) and move on...

If there were giants before the Flood, living at the same time as the ordinary-sized people, where are the fossils of these giant men who 'came in unto the daughters of men'? If gaps in the fossil record *prove* that evolution is false, then gaps in the fossil record *prove* that the Bible is lying, or (if I'm being more generous than I should be) is not 100% accurate.

You can't have it both ways.

Giants lived at the same time as man. And didn't the Flood kill everything? So where are these missing fossils?

You can't have it both ways.

An explanation for this failure to find fossils of giants would be that fossils are difficult to create, they only happen under certain conditions, and this makes them rare. Some animals *never* lived in conditions where it was possible for fossils to form.

This sounds logical, but there is a slight problem.

This is *exactly* the explanation that *evolutionary scientists* give for not finding the so-called 'missing links' (more properly they should be described as 'intermediate species'). Fossils are rare simply because it's so incredibly improbable that any animal will *ever* become a fossil.

So the very same arguments which Christian Creationists give to discredit evolution can also be used to discredit the Bible. If everything was killed in the Great Flood, we should be finding fossils of giants.

Unicorns are mentioned in the King James Version of the Bible, but Christian apologists will try and get out of that one by saying that, 'unicorn' was an incorrect translation from the Hebrew. We don't think it was really a unicorn now.

No shit, Sherlock. But why keep the word in the Bible at all if it's supposed to be the perfect word of God? The KJV Bible was used for *hundreds* of years before more modern translations came along. Was God happy to have the wrong words dotted around his Holy Book?

Here's another point: let's accept that the unicorns in the Bible aren't *real* unicorns, and the *dragons*, *behemoths* and *leviathans* in the Bible actually refer to dinosaurs.

What? Yes, Creationists believe that man and dinosaurs once walked the Earth at the same time, before the Flood. Noah loaded up two sheep, two goats, two elephants, then... two Tyrannosaurus rexes, two Velociraptors, two Pterodactyls... and so on.

Do I sense an unhealthy quantity of bullshit here? But, let's run with the fantasy...

We'll assume that the Flood killed all the other dinosaurs, all at once. So there would have been hundreds, probably thousands, of each of the very many types of dinosaurs that we know about.

So where are they?

Why do we more often than not only have *one* example of a particular dinosaur species? If they all died at once in the Flood, shouldn't we find *hundreds* of them? Most animals live in packs or family groups. At the very least we should be finding small herds of dinosaurs, surely?

Of course we don't, because the Flood is a fantasy. It's rubbish. If man walked with dinosaurs, how come we don't find human fossils in the same rock strata as the dinosaurs?

We find ancient human remains, that's true, but these are not fossils of the same age as the dinosaurs. Fossil bones are turned almost into rock over millions of years. Human bones that we find are not the same. They haven't had those millions of years, and are certainly not found under metres of sedimentary rocks.

Where did all the fossils go?

This is why you should never listen to Christians who talk about evolution. Many of the arguments they give for doubting the evidence of evolution can be used in exactly the same way to falsify the Bible.

If gaps in the fossil record prove that evolution is wrong, they also prove that the accounts of the Bible Flood are wrong. If the Bible is true, there should be *millions* of fossils, pile after pile of them, because if they all died under the same conditions, during the Flood, they should all have become fossils, all at the same time.

If there is only one fossil example of a species, where are all the others?

The answer is this: the Biblical Flood never happened. Fossils are scarce, and there are gaps in the fossil record, simply because fossilisation is so incredibly unlikely to happen to an animal when it dies. The odds of it happening are much, much longer than those for winning the lottery.

That is why there are gaps in the fossil record. That's why, even if giants ever existed, we may never find any fossils of them. The evidence we have, the fossils themselves, fits exactly with what we would expect to find if they had been preserved under sediment, which over millions of years became rock.

There will always be gaps in the record. We would not expect anything else. Assuming that life evolved gradually over billions of years, how many millions of generations of fossils would we have to find for there to be absolutely no gaps in the fossil record? We would probably have to find fossils of every single animal that ever lived.

And guess what, if we *did* find fossils of every single animal that ever lived, Creationists would just say, 'Ahah! Finding all those animals is evidence for the Flood! That proves the Bible is true!'

You obviously can't argue with Creationists. To them, evidence or lack of evidence is all the same, it's Biblical proof if it's there, and it's Biblical proof if it isn't. Some Christians would hold the Bible to be true even if someone uncarthed a time-lapse video showing every significant evolutionary event throughout the billions of years since life first emerged.

Just remember that this is the same Bible that has led to Christians believing in giants, walking on water, and trumpets making city walls fall down. And don't forget the prophecies: locusts shaped like horses, with long hair and big teeth, wearing crowns. Yes, God the magical zoo keeper is just waiting to try out some new animals on us, before he kills everything again and sends most of us to Hell.

Beats the Discovery Channel doesn't it?

More Biblical giants.

There were giants in the earth in those days; and also after that, when the sons of God came in unto the daughters of men. Genesis 6:4

And there we saw the giants... And we were in our own sight as grasshopper, and so we were in their sight. Numbers 13:33

The Emims dwelt therein in times past, a people great, and many, and tall, as the Anakims; Which also were accounted giants.
Deuteronomy 2:10-11

That also was accounted a land of giants: giants dwelt therein in old time... A people great, and many, and tall, as the Anakims; but the Lord destroyed them. Deuteronomy 2:20-21

For only Og king of Bashan remained of the remnant of giants; behold his bedstead was... nine cubits was the length thereof, and four cubits the breadth of it. Deuteronomy 3:11

And the coast of Og king of Bashan, which was of the remnant of the giants. Joshua 12:4

The valley of the son of Hinnom, and which is in the valley of the giants. Joshua 18:16

Goliath, of Gath, whose height was six cubits[1] and a span.
1 Samuel 17:4

---

[1] A cubit was anywhere between 18 and 21 inches, so Goliath would have been at least 9 feet tall.

39

God's Little Retirement Project

Fetch the pipe and slippers.

The Universe and all that's in it simply cannot be the main career choice for God. Caring for mankind looks suspiciously like a hobby. A big, complex, detailed hobby, I'll grant you that, but definitely a hobby.

Think of the people who set up model railways in their garage, or up in the attic. Those guys painstakingly construct entire scenes from the fascinating (but dull) history of rail travel. And not just the trains and the track, which of course have to be accurate down to the finest detail. They set up the landscape too, the environment. Trees, bushes, grass, rivers, hills, rocks, all of these have to be realistic, accurately scaled, immaculately constructed. Every brick in every building must look just so. Little model people and animals populate the countryside through which the trains will run. Oh yes, all these things and more are part of the life of the model railway enthusiast.

Isn't it obvious, then, that the whole of Creation must be a hobby for God? There is no way that this is his main line of work. You'd need true devotion to be dedicated enough to put the hours into something like this, and I can't imagine any Supreme Being willing to spend all his time fitting atoms together one by one. There's just no money in it.

It's obvious. God has retired. He has enough cash in the bank to be comfortable, the winter cottage near the lake is bought and paid for, and now he just wants to potter about, doing little jobs around the house, keeping himself busy with a hobby.

Creation is God's retirement project.

It's just a phase.

No model railway enthusiast could ever build a decent layout in six days. He'd have to cheat, he'd have to buy all the scenery pre-made, all the engines and carriages factory painted, probably sit down with a mail order catalogue and buy a huge list of components, and even *then* six days would be a struggle.

But on the seventh day, after cutting a few corners, leaving out a few areas he didn't have time to finish, and covering over one or two mistakes that were made along the way, he could finally play with his choo-choos.

Creation sounds like that kind of hobby. An impulse. A rush job. A phase that God was going through. God had no real interest in making everything individually, in taking care to make each detail perfect. So he bought a kit, fitted it together, flicked the switch, and started to play with his little toys.

Do you know how boring the people are who build model railways? Do you know how tedious it can be to have a conversation with someone who can talk about 'soldered rail joiners', 'the properties of Styrofoam when used for landscaping', and 'horn hook couplers versus knuckle couplers'? Very. Very. Boring.

Surely then it's more than probable that God's word will be just as tedious, just as yawn-inducingly boring. And it is. Just read the Bible – the evidence is all there.

The Universe is a botch job.

You can tell that God didn't have the patience to make things one by one. Some parts of Creation are really quite sloppy, from the very small to the very big. It's all shoddy, mass-produced work that could have been so much better if he'd really tried.

For one thing, most places in the Universe will kill life instantly, whether by extreme temperature (too hot, too cold), by radiation, or more generally by an absence of conditions which would allow any life to exist at all. Space is dark, cold and dangerous. God couldn't be bothered to fill it with nice, colourful, habitable 'things', so he just left it empty.

Galaxies collide, ripping each other apart. Stars form in a highly inefficient way – only a very small percentage of a gas cloud actually goes into the star, so most of the resources are wasted. And after all that they eventually burn out anyway, like a spent light bulb.

Our Sun is a star, and it too will inevitably burn out. There doesn't seem to be a fall-back plan, unless God decides to create another Sun and replace the bulb at the centre of our Solar System when it pops.

These things happen, and God lets them happen. Does he ever intervene? Does he even care that the stars he made blow themselves up?

This is bad design, wasteful design, which God could easily have corrected if he'd taken more care.

Earth? WTF?

Earth. Come on, this was *not* the latest factory model was it? God either bought a second-hand planet from a dodgy salesman, or he ordered a box of parts from eBay that turned out to be salvage stock from a warehouse fire. The Earth is *damaged goods*. It's a mess, all bent and broken, with bits of it sliding around making all kinds of trouble – earthquakes, volcanoes, tidal waves, and more.

The true model enthusiast would hang his head in shame at that unfinished landscape. Rocks, ice, desert? Human beings don't tend to flourish where the conditions are suitable only for killing most life forms. People can't even live on most of the planet because it's covered with water. Undrinkable water at that, which is hardly the best design feature on a planet where man needs *fresh* water to survive.

All God had to do was regulate the salt content (and any aquarium owner could tell you how), but no, he just dumped a bucket of chemicals in the oceans, stirred it up a little, threw in some fish, and pretty much left it as it was.

The climate is *really* messed up on a lot of the planet. All it takes is for a little more water than usual and the rivers flood (deaths), too little and there are famines (more deaths). Maybe a hurricane will flatten whole towns and villages (even more deaths). The electricity supply isn't even connected properly, what with all those bolts of lightning hitting the ground at random (you guessed it, still more deaths).

And it's not just mankind getting killed on a daily basis by God's bad design. 99% of all species that ever lived are now extinct. What happened to the dinosaurs? Did God knock over a cup of hot coffee and scald them all to death? If it was a huge asteroid, as we suspect, what was it doing up there in the first place? If you designed something like the Earth, wouldn't you make sure there were no multi-mega-ton *rocks* heading towards it on a collision course? Just for safety's sake?

It's this lack of care, this chaotic and haphazard construction of everything around us, that shows up the amateurish nature of God's Creation.

What was God *thinking* when he put the Earth together? It's a pile of crap, let's admit it. If this was your car you'd be ashamed to drive it down the street. In fact you'd be lucky to get it that far, and it would probably be headed straight to the crusher by now.

The (im)perfect human.

God loves us. He made us. So the Bible says. But we may as well have been built from cheap plastic kits for all the care he put into our construction. Look at all those diseases – major design faults, methinks. You can't tell me that a child with leukaemia was made that way on purpose. That would be barbaric, wouldn't it? God is probably just sloppy with the glue, and was in a hurry when he stuck together the prototype.

What's the story with hair falling out of our heads, but at the same time growing out of our noses and ears, as we age? That doesn't sound like intelligent design at all. Facial hair on women? Hmm.

Teeth falling out, brittle bones… could God not have found more durable materials than the ones he used for humans? After all, he managed to make the giant tortoise live up to a couple of hundred years, so why did mankind only get around 80?

It's not as if he didn't *try* to extend our lives. After all, the people in the Old Testament lived *much* longer, and Methuselah was well over 900 when he finally started pushing up the daisies. So did God lose interest? Did he get bored putting together well-made, durable humans, and settle for mass-produced cheap imports? It certainly looks that way.

Our batteries need re-charging every night, losing a third of our lives in sleep. What a waste. And we spend another large chunk of our days eating – compare that to reptiles and snakes who might eat once a month and be happy with it. Life would be so much more productive if we didn't have to sleep or stop for lunch. A missed opportunity if ever there was one.

Unlike some animals we can't see in the dark. Why did they get that ability and not us? Surely humans were supposed to be made in God's image, but does that mean God can't fly, or swim underwater for hours, or detect sounds from miles away? We are just second rate dolls, slapped together in a six-day rush, with no thought for durability, no real aptitude for living in the harsh environment that God made for us.

God is bored.

If this is God's hobby, his great retirement plan, it's obvious that he got bored. Far from being an intelligent designer, whoever built the Universe, and supposedly made every one of us, was sloppy, talentless, and lazy. He took no great pride in his work at all. Most of the Universe is empty and uninhabitable, most of the Earth would kill humans if you dropped them onto it without some kind of technology, and most humans have bodies which, far from being perfect likenesses of God, have bumps, lumps, growths and all manner of diseases and weird parts which frankly don't look at all nice, especially as we age.

It's as if the whole thing, the Universe and everything in it, evolved over billions of years to create all this variety, this diversity, warts and all. Why would anyone build something like this on purpose?

But that would mean that there is no God, and what kind of Universe would that be?

Why is the Bible So Complicated?

The word puzzle of God.

There's a reason most Christians don't read the whole of the Bible. It's not because it's so long, or because they don't have the time. Boredom? Well, no comment, but that's not it either. No, Christians don't read the Bible simply because it's so damned complicated.

What with all the olde English lingo, the confusing parables, metaphors, allegories, symbolism and other weird and wonderful 'stuff' that's in there, is it any wonder that you need a preacher to interpret it all? It's like telling a joke. If you tell a joke but nobody laughs because they didn't understand it, and you have to explain the humour behind the story, then it simply isn't funny. It's not a good joke.

By the same reasoning, if there's a passage in the Bible which takes two minutes to read, but then it needs an experienced preacher to give a thirty-minute explanation of its meaning, well... it wasn't a very good story was it?

In most churches, the preacher, priest, pastor, call him/her what you will, gives a sermon to the congregation every Sunday. The nature of Christianity is such that you can guarantee that this sermon will include one or more passages from the Bible, followed by an explanation of those passages. Or the preacher might tell his own modern-day story, and find a reading from the Bible which fits alongside it, perhaps using current events to interpret the word of God.

But why? Why is there the need for such sermons at church? Why does it need someone with knowledge, someone who has studied the Bible for many years, to stand up in front of the congregation and explain what God wants people to do?

Why do we need so many people to interpret the Bible in different ways? If God was so perfect, would he not guarantee that everyone could understand it in exactly the *same* way?

Pick a church, any church.

There are over 33,000 different types of Christian church, 33,000 denominations. They all follow Christianity and interpret the word of God, but all in different ways, some of them radically different from others.

How can some Christians believe that the Earth is only 6,000 years old, and yet others believe, as science tells us, that it was formed 4.5 billion years ago? Wouldn't God want us to know, in no uncertain terms, how old the Universe is?

Some Christian churches allow women preachers, but some actively forbid it. Wouldn't God ensure we understood which was right, given that he has a big, detailed book with his 'Word' on every page?

Many churches will not marry divorced people, but some do. Do those which won't allow this have some Biblical reason for such a prohibition? But if they do, why don't the churches which *do* allow re-marriage also take heed of this rule?

Why is religion open to interpretation? Why is it such a pick-and-mix affair? A little ban on contraception here, a pinch of misogyny there, and solemn prayer versus laying on of hands. It's rare to see the Pope dancing in the aisles and singing gospel music, so why do Baptist preachers, for example, favour this approach?

If the Bible was so easy to follow, there wouldn't be over 33,000 different Christian denominations. All churches would teach the same lessons, and preach in exactly the same way. The word of God would not be open to interpretation.

How can you be sure you chose the right denomination? You might be brought up as a Catholic, the biggest Christian sect of all, but the Evangelists don't even think that Catholics are Christian, and certainly differ widely in their doctrines. Who is right? Why doesn't the Bible make it clear?

If you are a Christian you have a one in 33,000 chance that you are right, that your brand of Christianity is the one that God intended people to follow when he passed on his words to the writers of the Bible. One in 33,000 isn't good odds. You'd think twice about putting even a small amount of money on a race horse with odds of 33,000 to one. It would have to be some kind of lame, disease-ridden donkey to have odds like that.

Which is more likely: that one of many the thousands of possible religions or sects is the 'right' one and the others are wrong, or that in fact *none* of them is right – they are *all* wrong? Would you stake your life, everything you own, on a bet where the odds are so heavily stacked against you?

And yet people do indeed spend their whole lives making that bet, gambling against the odds, wasting away their time on something which has such a small chance of being right. Even if Christianity is right, only one of the 33,000+ denominations can possibly be correct. Not to mention the 10,000 other religions in the world which might also be right. And 150 of those have over a million followers, so we're not talking about weird, rock-worshipping cults here.

Why do all these divisions exist? Why all these denominations? If the Bible were less confusing, there would be no need for any of them. There would be only one, and all Christians would belong to it.

Criticising God.

Fair enough, you could argue with some degree of certainty that all Christians go to church to praise God. It's clear that God loves worship. It's what keeps him happy and stops him killing (more) millions of people. That much, at least, we can work out from the Bible, and it's a part of religion which is pretty easy to understand.

But the sermons? The preaching? If the Bible was written properly, if it was meant to be easily understood, the person leading the service could just read directly out of the Bible and end it there. Isn't God all-powerful? Couldn't he have dictated the Bible to make it absolutely plain, without any room for debate, what he was trying to tell us? Why can't he just make it known what he wants us to do? Why all the convoluted stories? Why so cryptic? Just tell us what you want us to do, God!

Many church sermons are like classes in literary criticism. When a school's English class studies any literary work, the lessons include some criticism of the work, some analysis. The characters and plot are explored in order to think about what the author intended the story to say to its audience.

Should Christians be criticising God's word in this way? Isn't it 'The Word of God', ie not open to interpretation? God knew what he meant when he said the words, surely, so why is there now a problem with understanding what they all mean?

Never mind all the stuff about seed falling on stony ground or on thorny ground. Or the fishes and loaves. What does it all mean? Some of the parables have their own explanations alongside them, actually in the Bible, but these are themselves so cryptic that the *explanation* needs to be explained, and so yet again the preacher takes over and tells you what Jesus meant when he told the story.

If God just said what he wanted, there would be no doubt. The Bible should be a list of instructions, no more, no less. If, as the Christians would have us believe, the Bible is a book which shows moral guidance, then please, let us have some idea of the things we can or cannot do.

And make it simple, because don't forget, this is the God who as well as creating people of high intelligence (aka atheists) also created some real dim-wits, and they really need it spelling out to them, step by step.

Of course the Bible does have a list of instructions. Not just *a* list. *The* list. The Ten Commandments, given by God to Moses, which are supposed to guide us and keep us on the right path.

Ten? Is that it?

Where is the Commandment which says 'thou shalt not rape', or 'thou shalt not molest a child'? Coveting thy neighbour's wife is, according to the Ten Commandments, to be avoided, yet there is no mention of torture, incest, arson, pornography, kidnapping, vandalism, racism… but at least God tells us not to work on the Sabbath, so that's alright then. Obviously that is so much more important than 'thou shalt not punch an innocent man's face' isn't it?

The Bible was not written by God, it was written by men. The Bible is not interpreted by people who are touched by God, it is interpreted by individuals who follow their own agenda, or the agenda of the denomination of church to which they belong. The Bible is vague, so all things are possible. Anyone can take a passage from the Bible and interpret it in a way which fits their particular doctrine, the teaching of their church.

Why is the Bible So Complicated? 193

And the fact that the Bible is so complicated means that there will always be jobs for preachers, and nobody will ever completely understand the Bible. It isn't meant to be understood. It is there for preachers to interpret, to convince a room of people that this is what certain passages mean, and to enable weak-willed people to believe that their brand of Christianity is the right one, and all the other 33,000 denominations are getting it wrong.

If there is a God, why doesn't he make it clear what he means? Couldn't God simply make his words appear, in a clear, easy-to-understand, not-open-to-interpretation way? Why did the Bible need to be written by men?

Surely God doesn't need a pen? It's a man-made invention.

And so is the pen.

God Almighty's Genesis Diary – Day 6

Day 6 – Saturday

8:05 am

I've had a 'cease and desist' notice telling me the name 'Randochaosity' is already a trademark, registered to 'Zeus and Sons'. Meh. I might have known he'd have his finger in the pie somehow. Oh well, it's the least of my worries now. I have to re-stock the animal kingdom and that's going to take most of the morning.

11:10 am

Guided by my almighty wondrousness, I think the animals are just about there. I've got croaking, growling, roaring, mooing, purring and barking things all over the place. And crapping, naturally.

This evolution business (the name occurred to me while I was watching a couple of monkeys banging each other silly) is a piece of cake once you get the rough edges knocked out of the system. I'll be raking it in once I get this to market.

12:15 pm

Okay. Man. Hmm.

Naturally I will make him in my own image. After all you can't improve on perfection! I can't really rely on evolution to do the whole job – they'll all end up as sex mad as the chimps, and I really need them to spare some time to praise me. Hey, it's what I'm here for, and don't I deserve some respect?

1:30 pm

I ditched the first attempt. The Man had a four-foot penis and I didn't think that a Woman with breasts three times bigger than her head was very practical. I really much stop watching so much porn, it's starting to influence my work.

2:15 pm

I don't think I can make it exactly in my image. Given that I'm invisible, the 'Make It So' button had trouble knowing what 'all seeing' looked like, so it seems to have covered the whole thing in eyeballs. There's one advantage: nobody will sneak up on him in a hurry, but he looks like walking frog spawn, which is not how I see myself. Or at least not how I would see myself if I wasn't invisible.

3:20 pm

This is Man. And he's… okay. Four feet eight, chubby face, cheeky little grin and a nice shade of brown. Not bad. I need to impart some knowledge and wisdom into him because he keeps asking me, 'what'chu talkin' 'bout, God?', but I think I'll go with this, at least as a beta version.

3:55 pm

I needed a bit of a contrast for Woman, because I'm hoping that together they will make a handful of other races, so I decided to mix up the features a little. I went with a yellowish tint on the skin, big eyes, and for some reason the voice sounds a little gravely, but it's kinda growing on me. Nothing too extreme, nothing fancy.

Except the hair. My favourite colour, and I make no apologies for this: blue. Woman has blue hair, and that's how it's going to be. I've seen it and as always (I can't help it) it is good. I was having a bit of trouble keeping it up in the beehive style, but with a little bit of the old Godly razzle-dazzle, it's as vertical as Man's little winky.

Talking of which, I see they've met. Yes, they definitely like each other. A little bit too much if you ask me. Damn, have they been watching the dogs mating? That is not the way it's meant to happen.

Let there be a bucket of water!

4:45 pm

I called Man and Woman into the office, just to get a few things straight. Told them I am their God, they must worship and adore me, etc, etc. Eat anything you want but not the apples. Why not? Because I say so, that's why. No, sex with animals is not alright, and neither is sex with trees or rocks. Fruit? Hmm. Borderline. If it's all you've got, well, any port in a storm. Know what I mean?

Man wanted to know if he can have sex with other men. Sure, why not? Whatever floats your boat. All the other Gods allow it, and I'm pretty liberal minded as Supreme Beings go, so hump any other human and I'll turn a blind eye. Girl-on-girl, well perhaps I'll monitor the situation closely to form an opinion on that. Very closely. And often.

Incest? Well of *course* that's okay, otherwise how would two people populate the whole planet? Sooner or later someone is going to have sex with his sister, brother, grandma, something like that. That's the way it is.

I told them they can pretty much eat anything and everything, but again I don't recommend the rocks – most are not very nutritious.

5:15 pm

I dropped them off back at the planet, and was just turning to leave when Man said, 'So this is our planet now is it?'

'Yes,' I said. 'I give every plant and tree and fruit and bird and…'

'Okay, we get it. So we can do anything we want from now on?'

'Within reason, yes. Was there anything in particular you were planning to do now that you have the whole planet at your disposal?'

Man started looking a bit embarrassed when I asked that, but I insisted he told me what was on his mind.

'Well, it's sort of like this. Even though you say you are a God, I really don't have any definitive proof that you exist, you being invisible and all.'

Woman nodded. It started to look like they'd already talked this one through.

'And for all I know the voice that's in my head is just a psychotic episode brought on by the trauma of being created in a few hours from dust. That and looking like Gary Coleman.'

'But I assumed you were happy with your appearance,' I said.

Man looked up at Woman. Way up.

Woman looked down at Man. Way down.

Both said: 'Are you fucking serious?'

'But what's all this about proving I exist?' Worrying about their looks was one thing, but this was starting to get intense.

'Well, it's like this…' said Man.

'Yes?'

'You're not going to like it.'

'Come on, Man, out with it!'

Man shrugged and cleared his throat.

'I deny the existence of the Holy Spirit.'

Woman looked at him, then at me (or where she thought my disembodied voice was coming from), and nodded in agreement.

'I deny the existence of the Holy Spirit too.'

I looked at Man. I looked at Woman. They cowered, ready for me to smite them down and burn their quivering, helpless bodies into ashes, or send them to eternal torment in my (still on order) lake of fire.

'That's cool,' I said.

'?'

'Personally I can't stand the little fucker. He's been a pain in the ass since he joined the company, and I've got no faith in him myself. I was going to fire him anyway.'

Man and Woman collapsed into nervous laughter, relieved.

In retrospect their optimism was unfounded. I manifested myself as a snake-haired Medusa and turned them to stone. Always wanted to do that.

Bloody atheists.

5:55 pm

Well, I never thought I'd get it done in time, but there it is, minus the two I just executed, but they'd already had 45 kids so the population will build up pretty quickly now.

I'm off to bed, and tomorrow... a well earned rest.

42

God is Irrelevant, Religion is Not

The invisible man in the sky.

Let's assume that God exists, somewhere out there, and that he's watching over us. Far-fetched it may be, but for the sake of argument we will tentatively accept that he is either floating in the sky, as people used to think, or 'outside the Universe', which is what they believe now that science has pushed back our understanding of space and we know that Heaven isn't up in the clouds or beyond the Moon.

Wave to the skies because God is watching you.

And... so what? What use is he? What does he actually do to change your life, my life, anyone's life here on planet Earth? Anything?

Nothing. God does nothing. He doesn't appear in front of anyone. He doesn't send down his angels to whisper in people's ears. He doesn't call down from the clouds in a booming voice, telling us what to do. He doesn't broadcast on national TV, doesn't have his own talk show, has never made so much as a documentary. Radio? Not even that. Not so much as a five-minute spot on some back-water third-rate radio show in Gluesniff County. No podcasts, no YouTube accounts, no viral email campaigns.

In all of recorded history, God has only ever written one book, and you could probably argue that that was not entirely autobiographical – many authors had a hand in it. The copyright has long since expired so the Supreme Being isn't making any money on the deal. You'd have expected a sequel by now, but God obviously has writer's block.

God does nothing. Nothing at all.

Obviously the real reason for this hive of inactivity is that God simply isn't there. But if he was there, and for many people in the world that is the belief they have, how does God's inaction, his

God is Irrelevant, Religion is Not   199

lethargy, his inability or unwillingness to actually do something, affect our lives?

It doesn't. Since God does nothing, his existence or non-existence doesn't matter one bit. God is irrelevant.

As an atheist I know that if, tomorrow, I walk out into a busy street and a bus hits me, I will probably die. God will not save me. But as an atheist I also know that a Christian hit by the same bus, under the same conditions, will also probably die. God will not save a Christian any more than he will save an atheist.

Ask the magic bean.

Atheists don't pray, so naturally God doesn't answer any thoughts, or internal calls for assistance in a crisis, from atheists. Christians do pray. Oh, how they pray, but is there any evidence that God answers their prayers? Surprisingly, there is.

God answers the prayers of his followers in one of three ways:

1. Yes, I will grant your wish
2. No, you're out of luck this time
3. Maybe later, I'm busy right now

Unfortunately this system of 'miracle-working' is a little vague. Certainly if you lose your car keys and pray for God's help in finding them, you may well discover their whereabouts ten seconds later (a *yes* response) or they may never show up at all (a *no*), or you may give up looking but find them a week later, down the back of the sofa where they had fallen out of your pocket (God 'helped' you later when he had more time).

But was that really God's intervention? Did God push you towards the missing keys? Did he erase the mental block which prevented you from finding them without his 'help'? Of course not. God had nothing to do with it.

You could pray to a cup of coffee and get the same results. You could pray to the pages of this book for the answer to all your ailments and the reply will be the same: yes, no or maybe later. And how would you know the difference? If God can answer your prayers with 'no', what does that tell you about God's influence on the objects and events in the physical world around us? It tells us that even if there is a God, he does nothing to affect the result. Nothing at all. God is irrelevant.

Bob kills.

Let's invent a disease. We'll call it Bob's Syndrome. Bob's Syndrome is a disease of the lungs. Statistically, 90% of people who contract Bob's Syndrome will die. There is no known cure, but 10% of people, 1 in 10, do manage to live on.

10 people in a certain hospital ward have Bob's Syndrome. Their families all pray to God that their sick relative will live. However, 9 of the patients sadly die from their condition. Their families are distraught, funerals are arranged, bodies are buried.

For the family of the person who continues to live, however, this is a miracle. God answered their prayers! He held back Bob's Syndrome and is keeping their beloved relative alive. Proof, if ever it was needed, that the power of prayer is a force to be reckoned with.

Not exactly.

Statistically, one of the ten people in the ward would have survived anyway. That's the way such statistics work – a large pool of results is examined, the numbers added up, and a percentage is calculated to represent the likelihood, based on past experience, that any one patient would survive the onslaught of Bob's Syndrome.

The ten families could have prayed to the moon; the results would have been the same. Even after praying to Oprah Winfrey, 9 out of the 10 would still have died. Should we then blame Oprah for these deaths? Should we even blame God for the 90% death rate? Of course not. The Christians who pray and get a 'no' do not then condemn God for failing to help their sick relatives. And yet the 'winning' family claim a miracle, the hand of God taking control of the situation, answering their prayers.

This is a ridiculous assertion. God did not help in any way. Prayer does not help the sick and the dying. It does not stop accidents happening, or natural disasters killing innocent people. Natural forces cause tidal waves and earthquakes, and only serve to prove that God has no part in these events. Praying that you will be spared will not prevent your death when a 10-story building collapses on you, or when a hurricane rips up a tree and drops it onto the car you are driving.

If God has no part in natural events such as these, why pray to him? If he isn't killing people, he certainly isn't helping them live either. He does nothing. He helps no one. If God is there, he is merely watching, and most probably not even doing that. God is irrelevant.

What *is* relevant?

God plays no part in your life. He does nothing to affect the world around us. Then what is relevant to our daily lives?

Religion.

Religion affects everyone, whether theist or atheist. Religion is for people, and it is people who write down the religious rules, the codes by which the followers of that religion are compelled to live in a certain way. Religion takes a person who does not actually need God, because God does nothing for him anyway, and convinces him to live his life according to a set of religious codes. And it convinces the religious follower that others, those who do not follow the 'righteous path' ordained by the leaders of a particular religion or sect, are wrong, and should be punished. More than that, religion teaches that others *will* be punished, simply for ignoring God and not playing by God's rules... which are of course rules invented by humans.

This makes religion relevant to atheists. Atheists do not want to follow all the rules set out by religion. God is irrelevant to us, so why should the teachings of his followers be any more relevant? Maybe some of the teachings of religion are good. 'Treat others as you would have them treat you' is a very sensible idea. But you don't need God to tell you that. You don't need one of the Ten Commandments to remind you that killing is a bad thing. God's presence is not needed to convince anyone that you should take care of your loved ones, try to live a happy life, and be charitable to others where possible. Atheists know that.

But religion tells atheists that they are bad. It also tells other religions that they too are bad, and that they will all be punished, simply because they did not praise God in the correct way.

More importantly, religion is relevant because it can bring down negative consequences on those who do not share its ideals. If you do not believe that abortion, even when it would save the life of the mother, is an abomination and should be illegal, you may be actively persecuted by the religious activists who do. You may be attacked, verbally or physically, or even be killed for your opinion, by the very people who forget that 'do not kill' is a fundamental part of their God's teachings.

Your local community may isolate you if you are not a fully committed, church-going Christian. Tell them you're an atheist and you may become a social outcast. In this case religion is relevant – at the very least you could lose friends, or the respect of other family members, who cannot accept that, for you, God is irrelevant. Religion is therefore wholly relevant to atheists.

Religion may enter the political sphere. If the elected leader of your country tells you that God himself talks to him, and influences his words, his actions, his political decisions, you'd better believe that religion is relevant to you. You may be forced to live in a country where avenues for future scientific discovery are blocked, simply because religion and politics become tangled together. In some countries, you may even be compelled to fight in a war against people or groups whose religion differs from yours, and for no other reason. If you are killed in a war started in the name of God, you'd better believe that religion is relevant to you.

Living with religion.

Atheists are not able to live apart from religion. God may play no part in their lives, but religion will always be there. Most atheists will accept the restrictions, the limitations of their freedoms, placed on them by a religion which is not their own. For the most part, that is simply because it is easier to accept those conditions than it is to speak out or fight against them. Some atheists, however, are willing to break their silence, to try to change the notion that they should be bound by the rules of a religion which is not their own.

God is already irrelevant. Perhaps one day religion itself will be consigned to the same fate.

God's Hard Drive is Bigger Than Yours

God's amazing memory challenge.

How likely is it that there is a God watching everything in the Universe? Every particle, every part of space? Every galaxy, with billions of stars in each galaxy? Apparently God is watching everything in the Universe, and yet he is also able to individually read everyone's mind *simultaneously* and record their every action. That must take some doing.

Since God is all-knowing, he must know the future. But that means that he knows what everything has done, is doing, and will do, for every second of the Universe's existence. To do that he would need to have made a copy of every particle in the Universe and store it somewhere, again and again, one copy for every second of time, past, present or future, until the end of time.

How likely is that? Let's juggle some numbers, obviously some of which will simply be the best estimates from science, but the size of the results should reveal that even if we're wrong by several orders of magnitude, there will still be some pretty mind-boggling figures coming out of our calculations.

The figures speak for themselves.

Let's take one exact copy of the Universe per second. We'll give God an impressive compression algorithm and allow him to store everything in a millionth of its original size. So, every million seconds God would create a million new Universes, and fit them into the space needed for just one Universe.

A storage unit the size of the Universe would be required every million seconds (around 11.5 days), but we'll give God the benefit of the doubt and round that up to 12 days. That's fine, and we already know that God made the Universe in 6 days, so he could very easily make more of them, given twice as long. Except remember that he is making a *million* Universes in that time – one every second for a million seconds.

One year is approximately 31.5 million seconds. Let's assume that the Christian Creationists are correct and that the Universe was made 6,000 years ago and, as many believe, Jesus will return within the next 50 years. God therefore doesn't actually need to know what happens beyond that point, since time will end. 6050 years x 31.5 million seconds = 190,575 million seconds, but let's call it 190 billion for convenience.

If God knows everything which *has* happened, *is* happening and *will* happen, he makes copies, in whatever form, of the entire Universe, and every particle in it, one copy for each second of its existence: 190 billion copies of the Universe. These 190 billion copies are indexed and sorted for ease of access, presumably under the name 'Google Omniscience', and God is able to consult these records any time he wants. God knows the future. All of it.

Is God really all-knowing? Does it sound likely that God has some giant hard drive somewhere, with 190 billion copies of the Universe on it, presumably with a copy of Windows to keep the whole thing running smoothly?

Is the scale of this huge records facility possible? For an omnipotent (all-powerful) being, of course it is.

But the problem escalates. A second is a man-made unit of time. We have nanoseconds too. A nanosecond is a billionth of a second. Down at the atomic level, plenty of things can happen in a nanosecond. In one nanosecond, electricity will travel approximately 12 inches through a wire. This means that God has to know what is going to happen in every nanosecond, past, present and future. He must have a copy of everything, but this time a billion times more copies than we previously thought. One billion copies per second, or 190 billion billion copies of the Universe. All this so that God can be all-seeing.

And we only arrived at this figure because we assumed a low-end 6050 years. Science (real science, not Creationism) estimates that the Universe is actually 13.7 billion years old, something like 2.25 million times older than the Creationist view. After more multiplication we find that God needs to have over 400 million billion billion (the number 4 with 26 zeros after it) copies of the Universe, just to know the past, present and future of all things.

Then remember how big the Universe is – maybe 100 billion stars in our galaxy, the Milky Way, alone. Multiply that by a ball-park 100 billion galaxies in the Universe, and we can work out how many stars God has had to monitor, down to the sub-atomic particle level, for billions of years. And there are a *lot* of particles in a star, so the number of particles in 10,000 billion billion stars needs a lot of monitoring and recording.

Of course this is now getting ridiculous. Omnipotence and omniscience are becoming meaningless. God has turned into the busiest public records clerk ever, just so that he can be all-knowing.

God is not all-knowing. But if he's not all-knowing, he can't be all-powerful. And if he isn't all-powerful, he isn't God.

Atheist Poems for Christian Kids

Oven-Ready Religions

Four and twenty Christians
Were standing in a row
They thought that God would save them all
But now they're down below

Four and twenty Muslim men
Stood waiting in a line
They prayed to mighty Allah but
God burned them all this time

Four and twenty Jewish dudes
All walking to the gate
'Yahweh let us in,' they said
But Hellfire was their fate

Four and twenty atheists
Could not believe their luck
'Heaven's real, we're going in!'
But God said, 'Are you fuck!'

No Crib Required

Away in a manger
No crib for a bed
The little Lord Jesus
Never existed

The Hanging Nun

There's a nun hanging out of the window
And she's looking up into the sky
She said that she's talking to God, but
She didn't explain to me why

I can't see the God that she mentioned
She says that he's plain as the paint
On the window she stuck her head out of
She tells me he's there… but he ain't

The Evangelist's Nightmare

Oh Christian man, you remarkable Fundie
You make such a noise at your church on a Sunday
All praising the Lord and condemning the sinner
And all before driving on home for your dinner

But what do you do in your house late at night
When your hatred subsides and you turn out the light
In your dreams you see Jesus he's coming for you
For you are the one type of Christian that's 'true'

But this time is different, death comes and claims you
Your heart stops, you hear words from God and he names you
You're taken to Heaven, he shows you the way
They're carrying banners, they want you to play

But nothing on Earth has prepared you for this
As the angels fly by and they all start to kiss
And the only song playing is YMCA
For in Heaven there's one type of soul and that's gay

45

Christians Need Miracles More Than Atheists Do

Believe it or not.

Christians don't need proof that God exists, and that Jesus is going to come back to Earth one day. They just believe it. They have faith. Christianity is a belief and a faith that the things in the Bible are true, and that God, Jesus and the Holy Spirit are all real.

Atheists don't believe that. One of the things we have in common, perhaps the most important thing in fact, is that we have no belief in God. Not just the Christian God. Any god.

I could go through a whole list of mythical beings who were invented by various ancient peoples thousands of years ago, none of which are based on fact, all of whom sprang from superstition and the need to explain things when no other explanation was available. The Judeo-Christian God, the God of Islam, the Hindu Gods, and all the other gods which some people curiously still believe in, are just as imaginary as the Greek Gods or the Celtic Gods or the Egyptian Gods.

And as atheists we don't believe in any of them.

Without knowledge there is only agnosticism.

If you're an atheist *agnostic*, you don't believe in God but you also have no proof of that. And in fact it's exactly because such definitive proof does not exist that the word 'agnostic' really has no relevance. None of us *know* for certain. Some people believe in God, some people don't. Belief is an entirely separate thing from knowledge. None of us can prove either the presence or the absence of

God. We don't have that knowledge. We lack the knowledge. And of course agnostic means exactly that – without knowledge.

We all either believe or don't believe, but none of us really know. So what would it take for us to have that knowledge?

This had better be good.

I've seen a lot of conversations and discussions where religious people, from many different faiths, have called out the atheists and said things like, 'Even if God showed himself to you, you wouldn't believe he was real.' Or, 'What would it take to make you believe in God?'

This first one is easy. It's not true. If God showed up tomorrow, all atheists would become believers. It's as simple as that. I don't know a single atheist who wouldn't hold up his hands, and probably even kneel down, and say, 'We were wrong, there is a God'. Because if you can see God, and everyone else sees the same as you do, you can't deny the truth. It's called evidence. If we had enough evidence, we'd believe in God.

If you have enough evidence, you can believe in anything. That's what proof is all about – providing enough evidence so that no rational person would be able to believe anything else.

The second question was: what would it take to make you believe in God? Obviously, for people who are sceptical of these things, and atheists are an extremely sceptical bunch, it's going to take a lot for us to believe that there is a supreme being. A big head floating in the clouds and a booming voice shouting, 'hey you down there, look up, I want to talk to you. I am your God', well, that would be a great start. Just to break us in gently. But if that was it, pretty soon people would be blaming it on the government or China or Bill Gates, and they'd probably start to question what they'd seen. Maybe it was a big projector, with a huge sound system, or lots of little projections linked up over the Internet.

So perhaps God would have to appear in person and do a few miracles. Now plagues of locusts, or enormous hurricanes wouldn't do it, because we could explain those away as natural phenomena. It would have to be something spectacular, something which broke some of the fundamental laws of science. Something you know that nobody could do without divine power.

Something like lifting mountains, or making a city disappear. What about turning all the guns in the world into flowers? That would show that not only did he have almighty power but that he came in peace and loved everyone (except the ones with allergies of course – all those flowers).

For an atheist to believe in God, that is what it would take. If God made the Universe, then it should be no problem at all to simply prove to us that he exists. He can do anything if he's God, and if it's impressive enough atheists will believe in him, without question. If he appears on Earth and demonstrates miracles that even Penn and Teller can't do, it's game over for atheism.

Obviously, atheists are still waiting on that. I don't think it's going to happen. And no other atheist does either, because if you thought that it might, you'd obviously believe in God already.

We're all waiting for proof. So in the strict definition of the word we're all agnostic. We lack the knowledge which would make us believe.

Sceptical Christians are everywhere.

Atheists are often told by Christians that this is the wrong way to think of God. God isn't a cheap magician who is going to come down and turn the Earth orange, or pluck aircraft out of the sky, or turn water into wine (okay that last one was a bad example). But, more often than not, we will be derided by Christians and told that we should believe in God, have trust in him, have faith in him. Christians don't need big shows of strength, they have a personal relationship with him and they simple know he exists.

But that's not quite true is it? Christians need proof too. Christians, if they are honest with themselves, are almost as sceptical as atheists about the existence of God. And they are the most sceptical people of all when it comes to Jesus Christ.

Christians will tell you with great sincerity that they believe unquestioningly in Jesus Christ. But I'm here to tell you that they don't.

Christians Need Miracles More Than Atheists Do

All Christians believe that Jesus is coming back to Earth. They are waiting for him, and they say they will welcome this second coming of their saviour. But there's a problem. The Bible says:

> *There shall arise false Christs, and false prophets, and shall show great signs and wonders; insomuch that, if it were possible, they shall deceive the very elect*
> God (Matthew 24:24)

In other words, don't believe in everyone who calls himself Christ, not even the ones who show 'great signs and wonders'. Which means of course, that when Jesus comes back, the Christians are going to need proof. *Big* proof. Not just walking on water – I've seen that myself on TV. Fishes and loaves? Any magician who gives himself the name can make things appear and disappear, no problem. Bringing back the dead... well, we're getting a little more challenging now. But the point is, for someone, anyone, Christian or not, to believe that a person who says he is Jesus really *is* Jesus is going to take some doing.

So Jesus would have to do something like lifting mountains, or making a city disappear. What about turning all the guns in the world into flowers?

If that sounds familiar, it's because that's exactly the same level of proof that atheists would need to believe he was the son of God. Christians won't believe it either until *they* have definitive proof.

So the next time a Christian ridicules you for the amount of proof it would take for you to believe in God, and says that his faith is unshakeable and unquestionable, ask him how he'll know it's really Jesus when he comes back. And if he mentions angels trumpeting, the sun darkening, or the stars falling from Heaven, just point out that that's some pretty heavy duty proof he's looking for there. Couldn't he just... believe?

46

God is History's Biggest Torturer

Limited offer – ticket holders only.

Here are some facts and figures, some official statistics. According to the CIA World Factbook[1], as of July 2006 there were approximately 6.5 billion people in the world. That number is growing by 1.14% per year, which means that this time next year there will be around 75 million more people on the planet than there are now.

People die, obviously, and the death rate is currently 8.67 deaths for every 1000 people. So in other words over 56 million people will die in the coming year.

Statistically, one-third of those deaths will be Christians, because one third of the people today say they are Christian. So if you believe the message of the Bible is true, 18 million people, one third of the people who die, will ascend up to Heaven, enter the pearly gates and have a lovely time flitting from cloud to cloud on their new wings, playing the harp and trying to get Jesus' autograph.

About a fifth of the people who die, again according to the statistics, will be Muslims, and if they're right, if Allah really is the one true God, this time it will be the people who believed in *him* who are allowed up into Heaven, and although this time the numbers will be smaller, that's still 11 million more Muslims in Heaven every year.

Now you might look at those two religions and think how wonderful the God of Christianity or Islam is, giving eternal peace and happiness to millions of dead people. And let's face it, if you're dead your options are pretty limited, so the concept of a place where you're going to live forever and never feel pain or suffering does sound quite appealing.

---

[1] https://www.cia.gov/cia/publications/factbook/geos/xx.html

God is History's Biggest Torturer   213

On the other hand, welcoming all those people into Heaven is only *part* of God's big plan. His other plan is to torture and burn everyone who doesn't make the cut, in everlasting fire and torment, for all eternity.

Christians believe that anyone who is not a Christian will go to Hell, and Muslims believe pretty much the same – if you don't worship Allah you're in for a world of everlasting pain and suffering.

What this means is that the Christian God will consciously and intentionally condemn 37 million people each and every year to Hell, to roast in the fires and scream forever. 37 million people, all sent to the most excruciating torture imaginable, all for the crime of not believing in the right God. That's not just atheists, that's Muslims and Hindus, Buddhists, Jews, Sikhs and anyone else. If you're not a Christian, you're a crispy one.

It's obviously going to be a lot worse if the Muslim God is the right one. Only 11 of the 56 million get into Heaven, which leaves 80% of dead people who don't. So the wonderful Allah, the God of Islam, consciously and deliberately decides to torture and burn around 45 million new people, adding 45 million more to the total, each and every year.

Actually if you're an Evangelist you can probably reckon on there being 9 million more sent down to the flaming pit, because half of all Christians are Catholics, and of course Evangelists don't believe that Catholics are Christians at all, so they're going to fry with the rest of them. In fact Evangelism just shades out Islam as the sect/religion whose God will torture the most people in any given year: 46 million new torture victims every year if you're an Evangelist. Well done Evangelism!

It's ten times worse than you think.

Don't forget that this is just for one year. So in only 10 years from now 370 million non-Christians will be burning (which is about half the entire population of Europe), or 450 million non-Muslims (which is about half the entire population of Africa). That's in *ten* years.

In 100 years, when nearly everyone alive today will be dead, two thirds of the entire population of the planet, that is 4 *billion* people (or

5 billion if you follow Islam), will all be sent to Hell by God, simply because they did not believe in the *right* God.

It's not even that a lot of these people don't believe in God at all. They just believe in the *wrong* God. You might believe in the God of the Bible just as strongly as someone else believes in the God of the Qur'an, but if you do you probably won't be seeing that other person again after you die because one of you will be cast down into agony without end, having your skin burned up over and over again for millions or even billions of years. At least that's what the Bible and the Qur'an say will happen.

This is the reality of that all-loving, all-caring God that the major religions love so much. God condemns 37 or 45 *million* people (depending on which God it is) to endless torture every year. Why anyone who does that could ever get a reputation for being good is a mystery to me. Think about it. Are there really between 37 and 45 *million* people each and every year who have committed crimes so bad that they deserve to be tortured until the end of time?

So you don't even need to count up all the people God killed in the Bible. Just look at how many millions of people he is adding to the fire, each and every year.

But spare a thought for atheism. Atheists don't believe that *anyone* gets tortured after they die. If you're a Muslim you won't be cruelly punished for your beliefs if it turns out they were wrong. If you're a Christian, atheists won't even try to scare you into believing that you should change your ways and accept atheism, so that you can avoid burning in Hellfire.

Atheists want you to know that if we never change the mind of a single person, if all the Christians stay faithful to Christianity, all Muslims keep on praying to Allah, and all Hindus keep on doing whatever it is they do, nobody, zero, not a single person will suffer in fiery torment for all time once they are dead.

So if it was a choice, and it isn't because I don't believe in God, but if I had a choice, I doubt I would praise a God who, if you look at the numbers, causes more pain in the afterlife than peace. All because you didn't believe in him.

God Almighty's Genesis Diary – Day 7

> **Subject:** Universe Disabled: Inappropriate Content
> **From:** The Higher Power
> **Date:** In the Beginning
> **To:** God T Father Jr
>
> ### PanTheon | Manifest Yourself™
>
> **Dear Deity:**
>
> After being flagged by members of the PanTheon community and reviewed by PanTheon staff, the Creation below has been removed due to its inappropriate nature.
>
> **Dinosaurs, giants and unicorns**
>
> Due to your repeated attempts to upload inappropriate creations, your Universe has now been permanently disabled and your creations have been taken down. If you feel your Universe has been disabled in error, please contact us to explain why.
>
> Please refer to our Terms of Use and the Community Guidelines for more information on what Creation material is not permitted on the PanTheon.
>
> The Higher Power™

So it's come to this. After all I've done for this place they give me the old heave-ho. This is censorship, plain and simple.

I'll call my lawyer. I'll start a petition. No, wait. I'll get the other Gods to create all of my dinosaurs in their own Universes, to show the Company they can't step on my dreams. You can't make an omnipotent God and then ban him.

Screw the PanTheon. From now on there's just one God and I'm it.

This is not over. This is so not over.

Printed in the United Kingdom
by Lightning Source UK Ltd.
124520UK00001B/347/A